MARK ANTONY & CLEOPATRA

MARK ANTONY & CLEOPATRA

Cleopatra's Proxy War to Conquer Rome & Restore the Empire of the Greeks

By Martin A. Armstrong

gatekeeper press™
Tampa, Florida

Mark Antony & Cleopatra:
Cleopatra's Proxy War to Conquer Rome & Restore the Empire of the Greeks

Published by Gatekeeper Press
7853 Gunn Hwy., Suite 209
Tampa, FL 33626
www.GatekeeperPress.com

Library of Congress Control Number: 2023943854

ISBN (hardcover): 9781662942570
ISBN (paperback): 9781662942587
eISBN: 9781662942594

Dedication

I would like to dedicate this work to my parents, Martin and Ida, who always inspired me to learn about and explore history. I would also like to dedicate this to Milton Friedman for inspiring me that what I learned as a trader was vital to the understanding of economics. And last, but not least, Lady Margaret Thatcher for her deep understanding of politics and how nothing really ever changes throughout the centuries.

Contents

Preface

**Benjamin Franklin
(1706-1790)**

First Edition The History of the Decline and Fall of the Roman Empire, by Edward GIBBON

IN 1776, EDWARD Gibbon (1737–1794) published his book, *The History of the Decline and Fall of the Roman Empire*. This work laid the groundwork of the American Revolution, following in the footsteps of Rome overthrowing their Tarquin king in 509 BC and establishing the Roman Republic. It was the final Battle of Actium, between Mark Antony (83-30 BC) and Octavian (63 BC-14 AD), that truly ended the Republic and gave birth to Imperial Rome. This coinage we are about to explore is of profound historical importance for it also involved an attempted coup funded by Cleopatra VII (70/69–30 BC; ruled 50-30 BC) to restore the Greek Ptolemy Dynasty of Alexander the Great (336-323 BC) to rule Rome. It was not simply a love affair.

Alexander III of Macedon *"The Great"*
(356 – 323 BC)

We must understand that the frailties of human nature always decide the fate of all nations. No matter what form they may take, in the end, they will always seek to preserve and expand their own power. This struggle even takes place to this very day as agencies in the U.S. compete against each other, such as the Securities & Exchange Commission

(SEC) versus the Commodity Futures Trading Commission (CFTC). It has been that competition which resulted in sending funds management offshore—establishing the Hedge Fund community— for domestically, if you obey the laws of the CFTC, you go to prison under the laws of the SEC.

When the United States Constitution was finally completed, an old wives' tale claimed that when Ben Franklin (1706-1790) was leaving the convention, he was stopped and asked, "What kind of government do we have?" He responded, "A republic, if you can keep it."

It has often been said that the best form of government is a benevolent dictatorship. Perhaps the reason some have reached that conclusion is because a benevolent dictator is beyond reproach—he cannot be bribed. At the time of the founding of the United States, many were deeply influenced by the knowledge emerging from history about the Roman Republic thanks to Edward Gibbon's book, also published in 1776. The American and French Revolutions were against monarchies, and they saw this as following the example of the Romans.

Nevertheless, the idealism which many believed existed within the Roman Republic overlooked its fatal flaw. No form of a republic has ever survived throughout history, for those pretending to represent the people are easily bribed. In France, this is the Fifth Republic established on October 4, 1958.

As we will explore, this idea that a one-world government will prevent war is absurd. Even a quick overview of Roman history reveals that numerous civil wars and revolutions took place. The propaganda hurled at Julius Caesar (100-44 BC) came from the fake news written by Cicero (106-43 BC) who, unfortunately, our Founding Fathers believed; they did not explore history in-depth to see that the Roman Republic became a vile oligarchy. Even Cato the Younger (95-46 BC) was the promoter of corruption and war. Nobody seemed to ask, when Caesar crossed the Rubicon, why did the people cheer, and the oligarchs of the Senate flee to Asia? This very coin issued by Caesar to pay the troops said it all—an elephant trampling the corrupt Senate, represented by the dragon-like serpent.

ORDER OF THE CINCINNATI
signed by George Washington

We have a republic; not a democracy as our politicians pretend. We have no right to vote on anything directly, including war or being drafted for war. A republic is a "representative" form of government, which is prone to bribery and individual self-interests. Thomas Jefferson (1743-1826) was in Paris when the Constitution was being drafted. On September 1, 1785, he sent a list of references to James Madison (1751-1836) to be used for forming the United States.

At the time of the founding of the United States, the emerging popular research concerned Rome. Here is an Order of the Cincinnati which was founded by George Washington (1732–1799; President April 30, 1789–March 4, 1797). He was inspired by the story of the famous Roman dictator Lucius Quinctius Cincinnatus (519–430 BC). He was an aristocrat and statesman who served as consul in 460 BC and dictator in 458 BC, as well as 439 BC, which made him a model of integrity and virtue.

The Romans regarded Cincinnatus as a hero. When Rome was invaded, he was called to serve as dictator, which was an office of one year. He defended the nation and resigned two weeks later after defeating the rival tribes of the Aequians, Sabines, and Volscians. His immediate resignation of power demonstrated his integrity and lack of personal ambition. Washington would not accept the office of president until he had resigned as military leader and returned to private life. The Founding Fathers were deeply impressed with the battle of Rome against its Tarquin king, which gave birth to a Roman Republic. Unfortunately, as we are experiencing now, all republics devolve into oligarchies and exploit the people.

Ben Franklin, on one occasion, was dining at a Paris restaurant and learned that Edward Gibbon was there as well. Franklin invited Gibbon to his table, but Gibbon refused, remarking that since he was loyal to King George III (1760-1820), he wouldn't speak with a rebel like Franklin. In reply, Franklin reportedly said that if Gibbon ever wanted to write a history of Britain's decline and fall, he would provide ample materials. This illustrates the contrast of the period.

George Washington's Order of the Cincinnati

Nevertheless, everything the Founding Fathers did was to accept the model of a Republic from Rome, not a Democracy from Athens, where the people had a direct vote. Keep in mind that they were making the transition to overthrow a monarchy, so Rome served as the inspiration. That transition was monumental.

Edward Gibbon's account of the crimes, follies, and misfortunes of the Romans was very influential on the revolution against monarchy during the eighteenth century. In his *Memoirs of My Life*, published in 1796, Gibbon explained:

"It was at Rome, on the 15th of October 1764, as I sat musing amidst the ruins of the Capitol, while the barefoot friars were singing vespers in the Temple of Jupiter, that the idea of writing the decline and fall of the city first started to my mind."

During the Middle Ages, the Roman Forum was the grazing grounds for animals. Edward Gibbon wrote the best epitaph:

"Her primeval state, such as she might appear in a remote age, when Evander entertained the stranger of Troy, has been delineated by the fancy of Virgil. This Tarpeian rock was then a savage and solitary thicket; in the time of the poet, it was crowned with the golden roofs of a temple, the temple is overthrown, the gold has been pillaged, the wheel of Fortune has accomplished her revolution, and the sacred ground is again disfigured with thorns and brambles.

The hill of the Capitol, on which we sit, was formerly the head of the Roman Empire, the citadel of the earth, the terror of kings; illustrated by the footsteps of so many triumphs, enriched with the spoils and tributes of so many nations. This spectacle of the world, how is it fallen! how changed! how defaced! The path of victory is obliterated by vines, and the benches of the senators are concealed by a dunghill.

Cast your eyes on the Palatine hill, and seek among the shapeless and enormous fragments the marble theatre, the obelisks, the colossal statues, the porticos of Nero's palace: survey the other hills of the city, the vacant space is interrupted only by ruins and gardens. The forum of the Roman people where they assembled to enact their laws and elect their magistrates, is now enclosed for the cultivation of pot-herbs, or thrown open for the reception of swine and buffaloes. The public and private edifices that were founded for eternity lie prostrate, naked, and broken, like the limbs of a mighty giant, and the ruin is the more visible from the stupendous relics that have survived the injuries of time and fortune."

There has often been a debate among scholars that the founders of the United States did not use Rome as their inspiration. They claim it served only as a referral in a post hoc confirmation of their biases that they extracted from history to justify their predetermined conclusions. That was not plausible when Jefferson sent reference materials to Madison in 1785. Making such arguments seems to be the pastime of people who never want to look at the facts and always try to manipulate the past to fit their current agenda. We will see this is also the case with the claims that Cleopatra was Black to further a modern woke agenda.

John Adams (1735-1826)
President (1797–1801)

Thomas Jefferson (1743-1826)
President (1801-1809)

Jefferson's letter to John Adams on December 10, 1819, confirmed he listened to the ancient "fake news" about Cicero against Julius Caesar (100-44 BC).

"I have been amusing myself latterly with reading the voluminous letters of Cicero. they certainly breathe the purest effusions of an exalted patriot, while the parricide Caesar is left in odious contrast. when the enthusiasm however kindled by Cicero's pen & principles subsides into cool reflection, I ask myself What was that government which the virtues of Cicero were so zealous to restore, & the ambition of Caesar to subvert? and if Caesar had been as virtuous as he was daring and sagacious, what could he, even in the plenitude of his usurped power have done to lead his fellow citizens into good government? I do not say to restore it, because they never had it, from the rape of the Sabines to the ravages of the Caesars."

Thomas Jefferson to John Adams, 10 December 1819

To John Adams
Monticello Dec. 10. 19.

Dear Sir

 I have to acknolege the reciept of your favor of Nov. 23. the banks, bankrupt law, manufactures, Spanish treaty are nothing. these are occurrences which like waves in a storm will pass under the ship. but the Missouri question is a breaker on which we lose the Missouri country by revolt, & what more, God only knows. from the battle of Bunker's hill to the treaty of Paris we1 never had so ominous a question. it even damps the joy with which I hear of your high2 health, and welcomes to me the consequences of my want of it. I thank god that I shall not live to witness it's issue. sed haec hactenus.—I have been amusing myself latterly with reading the voluminous letters of Cicero. they certainly breathe the

Thomas Jefferson
(1743 - 1826)

purest effusions of an exalted patriot, while the parricide Caesar is left in odious contrast. when the enthusiasm however kindled by Cicero's pen & principles subsides into cool reflection, I ask myself What was that government which the virtues of Cicero were so zealous to restore, & the ambition of Caesar to subvert? and if Caesar had been as virtuous as he was daring and sagacious, what could he, even in the plenitude of his usurped power have done to lead his fellow citizens into good government? I do not say to restore it, because they never had it, from the rape of the Sabines to the ravages of the Caesars. if their people indeed had been, like ours, enlightened, peaceable, and really free, the answer would be obvious. 'restore independance to all your foreign conquests, relieve Italy from the government of the rabble of Rome, consult it as a nation entitled to self government, and do it's will.' but steeped in corruption vice and venality as the whole nation was, (and nobody had done more than Caesar to corrupt it) what could even Cicero, Cato, Brutus have done, had it been referred to them to establish a good government for their country? they had no ideas of government themselves but of their degenerate Senate, nor the people of liberty, but of the factious opposition of their tribunes. they had afterwards their Titusses, their Trajans, and Antoninuses, who had the will to make them happy, and the power to mould their government into a good and permanent form. but it would seem as if they could not see their way clearly to do it. no government can continue good but under the controul of the people: and their people were so demoralised and depraved as to be incapable of exercising a wholsome controul. their reformation then was to be taken up ab incunabulis. their minds were to be informed, by education, what is right & what wrong, to be encoraged in habits of virtue, & deterred from those of vice by the dread of punishments, proportioned indeed, but irremissible; in all cases to follow truth as the only safe guide, & to eschew error which bewilders us in one false consequence after another in endless succession. these are the inculcations necessary to render the people a sure basis for the structure of order & good government. but this would have been an operation of a generation or two at least, within which period would have succeeded many Neros and Commoduses, who would have quashed the whole process. I confess then I can neither see what Cicero, Cato & Brutus, united and uncontrouled, could have devised to lead their people into good government, nor how this aenigma can be solved, nor how further shewn why it has been the fate of that delightful country never to have known to this day & through a course of five & twenty hundred years, the history of which we possess one single day of free & rational government. your intimacy with their history, antient, middl[e] & modern, your familiarity with the improvements in the science of government at this time, will enable you, if any body, to go back with our principles & opinions to the times of Cicero, Cato, & Brutus, & tell us by what process these great & virtuous men could have led so unenlightened and vitiated a people into freedom & good government, et eris mihi magnus Apollo. cura ut valeas, et tibi persuade carissimum te mihi esse.

Th: Jefferson

In matters of war, the first casualty is always the truth. History is also written by the victor. Take Thomas Jefferson, for example. He is a hero of the American Revolution, but a traitor to the British. The British sent a specific army to capture just one man—Jefferson. He was warned, and escaped before they arrived at his home.

British Token - the End of Pain

Thomas Paine
(1737–1809)

You always have both sides putting out their propaganda. Thomas Paine (1736–1809), who wrote *Common Sense*, inspiring the American Revolution, was the subject of British political tokens calling for his death.

Every article you read in West about Ukraine says that Russia is losing, and it is weak. This is a strategy to make it sound like the West is winning and can destroy Russia with no problem. This is simply how propaganda during time of war functions today, just as it did in ancient times.

Iraq had weapons of mass destruction that never existed; Vietnam never attacked us; and the sinking of the Lusitania took place even after Germany took an advertisement in the New York papers warning that the U.S. was using passenger ships to move weapons secretly and that they would sink it.

TRAVELLERS intending to embark on the Atlantic voyage are reminded that a state of war exists between Germany and her allies and Great Britain and her allies; that the zone of war includes the waters adjacent to the British Isles; that in accordance with formal notice given by the Imperial German Government, vessels flying the flag of Great Britain, or of any of her allies, are liable to destruction in those waters and that travellers sailing in the war zone on ships of Great Britain or her allies do so at their own risk.

IMPERIAL GERMAN EMBASSY

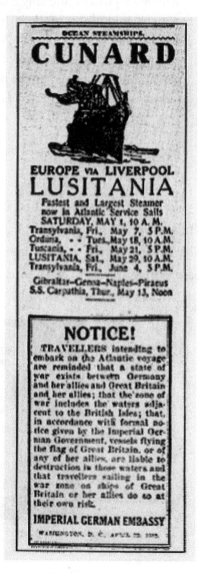

Washington, D. C., April 22, 1915

Truth always lies behind the headlines and in ancient times, it was no different. The CIA sought to kill Americans and blame that on Cuba to justify an invasion. President Kennedy rejected that proposition. It has been declassified as Operation Northwoods[1].

Just as the U.S. is using Ukraine as a proxy war to destroy Russia, Cleopatra used Mark Antony to carry out her proxy war to conquer Rome and reestablish the empire of Alexander the Great. Nothing is ever what it seems in time of war.

---

1   https://en.wikipedia.org/wiki/Operation_Northwoods

Introduction

WHAT WE ARE about to explore is history confirmed by the coinage revealing that Cleopatra VII was not engaged in some love-at-first-sight affair with Mark Antony. Cleopatra was by no means naïve nor stupid; she was not a Black African to satisfy this new WOKE agenda.

Roman Silver Denarius - Civil War

Julius Caesar
(100 - 44BC)

Pompey Magnus
(106 – 48BC)

ArmstrongEconomics.COM

Cleopatra was cunning and certainly very calculating. She engaged in a manipulation of Antony to create a proxy war with the intent to conquer Rome. She knew what she was doing, and she was well aware of her place in the history of the Macedonian empire of Alexander the Great (356-323 BC). Her first attempt to entice a Roman was not even Julius Caesar (100-44 BC). She also appears to have gone after Pompey the Great's (106-48 BC) son.

Mark Antony, 44-30 BC
Legionary Denarius (3.68 grams), military mint (Patrae?), 32-31 BC
Galley right/LEG VI Aquila between two signa
Crawford 544/19.

The legionary denarii of Mark Antony (83-30 BC) are probably the most significant issue of coinage ever struck during the period of the Roman Empire from a monetary perspective. The reason I have attributed such a title to the otherwise unimpressive series of coinage is the fact that they remained in circulation for over 200 years. Even more than 100 years following their issue, they still accounted for about 20% of the entire money supply of the Roman Empire. That, in and of itself, is quite incredible, to say the least.

Cleopatra VII
(51 - 30BC)
Æ Drachm of Egypt (16.84 grams)

In addition, the purpose behind the issue was intimidation funded by Cleopatra VII (70/69–30 BC; ruled 50-30 BC) Each legion at that time would have the strength of about 5,500 men. Therefore, issuing coinage denoting each legion loyal to Antony was projecting that his forces were overwhelmingly superior. The vast total amount of coins struck was in excess of 25 million denarii. So, while people have debated for decades that some of the legionary coins must be fakes after legion XXIII, that is not necessarily true. They overlook the entire point of issuing this series of legionary Denarii—propaganda.

There are clearly genuine coins displaying legions greater than XXIII. What has been overlooked is the propaganda factor. Before any battle, each side seeks to access the size of their opposing army. The very purpose of these coins was propaganda and intimidation to imply that the majority supported Antony, not his rival, Octavian.

Servius Sulpicius Galba, who served in the 12th Legion during the Gallic Wars of Julius Caesar (100-44 BC), has provided a record that he confronted Legion XXXV, led by Mark Antony. Servius

"The Death of Cicero" by François Perrier

Cicero was a vile man. He contrived to pit Octavian against Mark Antony to seize control of the corrupt Senate. His hatred of Antony, in particular, was legendary. He even suggested that Antony married Fulvia, his first wife, for her money, making her a devoted enemy. Cicero had also conspired to prevent Octavian from rising to power. Fulvia defended Antony from Cicero's attacks and ended up loathing his very devious character.

Second Triumvirate

Second Triumvirate
IONIA, Ephesus 43-33 BC. Æ18
Struck 40-39BC
Octavian, Mark Antony, & Lepidus/Facing Artemis Ephesia

ArmstrongEconomics.COM

THE SECOND TRIUMVIRATE was formed between Octavian (63BC–14 AD), Mark Antony (83-30 BC), and Marcus Aemilus Lepidus (89-12 BC). It was now abundantly clear that the inherent corruption that seized control of the Roman Republic was like a cancer eating everything from within. It was Cicero (106–43 BC) and his utter hatred of Julius Caesar (100-44 BC), who was a member of the Populares (man of the people), attempting to drain the political swamp in Rome.

Cicero connived against Mark Antony and Octavian, along with all their supporters, in a desperate attempt to retain the control and corruption of the Senate under the banner of the Republic. This behind-the-scenes backstabbing forced Octavian, Antony, and Marcus Lepidus to band together forming the Second Triumvirate on November 27, 43 BC with a term of five years. It was renewed in 37 BC for another five years and expired in 32 BC.

At first, Antony and Lepidus needed to confront Octavian. The Senate had actually instructed Octavian to hand over control of all the troops to Decimus Brutus (81–43 BC), the distant cousin of the notorious assassin Marcus Junius Brutus, but he refused. This had to raise suspicions in Octavian's mind. Antony and Lepidus met with him on an island in a river, possibly near modern-day Bologna, with their armies lined along opposite banks of the river in a classic confrontation.

This is when they formed the Second Triumvirate. They relied on the law to legalize their pact with the name of Triumvirs thereby assuming Consular Power under the *lex Titia* of 43 BC (Law of Titia). They had circumvented the office of consul appointed by the Senate and formally declared the end of the Republic as it had been known assuming five-year term of power.

Cicero's hatred blinded him to the possibility of these three men joining forces. They now possessed overwhelming superiority. Decimus Brutus's troops simply deserted him in the face of such odds and the lex Pedia declaring all the assassins to be criminals. This handed complete control of the Western provinces to the triumvirs.

Marcus Tullius Cicero
(106–43BC)

Cicero himself had made it very clear that the assassination of Julius Caesar was necessary and sought the extermination of all those who had supported Caesar. Antony pursued his political enemies, especially Cicero, who had openly criticized him for abusing his powers as consul after Caesar's assassination.

Fulvia
Third wife of Mark Antony
mother-in-law of Augustus

In the end, Cicero thus marked himself as a conspirator. Cicero was caught on December 7, 43 BC and beheaded by two of Antony's men for his continued political crimes of manipulating events for personal gain.

Fulvia's revenge against Cicero was noted by the historian Cassius Dio (c. 165–235 AD), describing the joy with which she pierced the tongue of the beheaded Cicero with her golden hairpins. This was her final revenge against Cicero's power of speech.

First Triumvirate (59-52BC)

Marcus Licinius Crassus
(115 – 53 BC)

Gaius Julius Caesar
(July 12th, 100 BC – March 15th, 44 BC)

Gnaeus Pompeius Magnus
(106 – 48 BC)

The actual First Triumvirate between Julius Caesar, Gnaeus Pompey, and Marcus Crassus, was different. This one was formally constituted. In truth, this marginalized the consuls and the Senate; in that respect it was a prelude to the fall of the corrupt Republic. The Second Triumvirate's legal life span being only for five years, it began with Lepidus in possession of both the provinces of Hispania (Spain), along with Narbonese Gaul (France).

Strategically, Marcus Aemilius Lepidus (89-12 BC) also agreed to hand over seven of his legions to Octavian and Antony to continue the battle against the assassins—Brutus and Cassius—which proved to be a fatal mistake. In the event of a defeat, Lepidus's territories would provide a fallback position. Lepidus was

Marcus Aemilius Lepidus
(89 - 12BC)

to become consul and was confirmed as Pontifex Maximus (high priest). He would assume control of Rome while they were away. When we look at the coinage produced, we see that the gold coinage of Lepidus is exceptionally rare. Most surviving gold coinage is that of Mark Antony and Octavian, suggesting that indeed Lepidus was a minor consideration in this Second Triumvirate.

Mark Antony   **Octavian**

Marcus Antonius & Marcus Lepidus
AV Aureus Second Triumvirate
© Trustees of the British Museum

Obviously, Lepidus's handing over his legions consigned him to an insignificant role in the Second Triumvirate. Nevertheless, by yielding his legions to Octavian and Antony, he also secured them the defeat of both Brutus and Cassius. Lepidus did agree to Antony's view that they should seize Cicero in revenge for the Philippics. For it was Cicero who was the mouthpiece of the oligarchs and the fake news.

Then there was Sextus Pompey (c. 67 – 35 BC), the last surviving son of Pompey the Great (c 67-35 BC), who saw the opportunity in the confusion following the assassination of Caesar and moved to seize Spain. Previously, when Caesar crossed the Rubicon, it was his older brother Gnaeus Pompey (75-45 BC) who fled Rome with their father and the corrupt senators to Asia. In both cases, they issued coinage to pay their troops with the portrait of their father.

Octavian renewed the conflict against Sextus as soon as he could assemble an army while Antony headed East. Sextus and Octavian both accused each other of violating the terms of the Pact of Misenum, which was a treaty to end the naval blockade of the Italian Peninsula during the Sicilian revolt. The pact was signed in 39 BC between Sextus and the Second Triumvirate.

Sardinia defected to Octavian and that was the final straw. Sextus defeated Octavian in the naval battle of Messina 37 BC and retook Sardinia. Octavian

Sextus Pompeius Magnus Pius
(c. 67 – 35 BC)
Portrait of Sextus Pompey/facing his father Pompey the Great
AV Aureus (7.8 grams)
ArmstrongEconomics.COM

then turned to his friend Marcus Vipsanius Agrippa (63-12 BC), who was a very talented general. Lepidus had raised fourteen legions in his African provinces to help defeat Pompey. It was for this confrontation that Sextus began to issue coins with his father's portrait in gold and silver to raise support among his father's followers.

Marcus Vipsanius Agrippa
(c.63–12BC)
ArmstrongEconomics.COM

Octavian then turned to the noted general Marcus Vipsanius Agrippa (c. 63-12 BC) and Titus Statilius Taurus, who had been a supporter of Antony. It was Antony who sent him to aid Octavian against Sextus Pompey in 37 BC. This was when Lepidus also raised fourteen legions in his African provinces to help defeat Pompey.

In 36 BC, during the Sicilian revolt, because Lepidus raised fourteen legions, this gave Octavian the excuse he needed to remove Lepidus from power. After the defeat of Sextus Pompey, Lepidus stationed his legions in Sicily and a dispute arose over whether he or Octavian had authority on the island.

This was when Lepidus began to see that Octavian was treating him as a subordinate and certainly not an equal member of the Triumvirate. Lepidus tried to negotiate, suggesting that Octavian could have Sicily and Africa, if he agreed to return Spain and Gaul to Lepidus. Octavian accused Lepidus of attempting to usurp power and fomenting a rebellion. Lepidus's legions in Sicily then bought the propaganda and defected to Octavian; thereby, Lepidus was compelled to submit. Then Octavian stripped Lepidus of all his offices on September 22, 36 BC except that of Pontifex Maximus.

It was clear that Octavian was seeking to grab all power. He sent Lepidus into exile in Circeii. After the

Marcus Aemilius Lepidus & Octavianus
AR Denarius
ArmstrongEconomics.COM

Battle of Actium, Lepidus's son was said to have been in a conspiracy to assassinate Octavian, who ordered him to be executed. Octavian always treated Lepidus with contempt. He did allow him to return to Rome, only to participate in some Senate votes. He died peacefully in exile.

Cleopatra's Proxy War with Rome

Cleopatra VII
(Born 69BC - died 30 BC)
(Bust in the Altes Museum)

CLEOPATRA VII PHILOPATOR (70/69–30 BC) has often been the subject of debate. For whatever reason, people have tried to claim that Cleopatra was Black, probably to embellish a view that Africans were not part of important history. Manipulating history to satisfy modern prejudice is probably the greatest crime against all humanity. Without understanding our true history, we will never be able to comprehend the risks that await us in the future.

Cleopatra was not Black simply because she was in Northern Africa. When Alexander the Great (356–323 BC) died, his empire was split among his generals. Egypt went to Ptolemy I Soter (c. 367BC–282 BC). Cleopatra knew her place in the Greek world and was out to even the score against Rome—this upstart empire.

Ptolemy I Soter
(b 367BC; King of Egypt 305-283BC)

Cleopatra VII
(70/69 – August 10 th, 30 BC)
The Herculaneum Portrait

There is a first century portrait painted of Cleopatra that has survived in the ruins of Herculaneum, buried in the eruption of Vesuvius along with Pompeii in 79 AD. This posthumous portrait of Cleopatra VII shows that she had red hair. This matches the image from her coins and busts showing distinct facial features. She is also pictured wearing a royal diadem and pearl-studded earrings. This distinguishes her as royalty.

Anyone who has worked in the Middle East and has knowledge of Iranians knows that the striking difference one first notices is that they often have red hair. At first glance, one would think they were Irish also with very white skin. There had been a Celtic movement south after 2200 BC which included a migration into Iran. Thus, Iranian-related ancestry arrived by the mid-second millennium BC. This would certainly account for the red hair one encounters in that region.

There was perhaps a sense of prejudice by the elite Greeks against those who they conquered which did not turn simply on skin color. It was more about being Greek, which was seen as superior race. Adding to this, there was a custom in Egypt among all classes in society that you were fortunate to have a sister to marry for that was one means of keeping the wealth within the family.

A 2015 study of the royal Egyptian mummies that predated Ptolemy shows that there was extensive inbreeding among the ancient Egyptians. The study published in the *American Journal of Physical*

Anthropology, conducted by Frank Rühli, Director of the Institute of Evolutionary Medicine at the University of Zurich, and colleagues, involved 259 Egyptian mummies, both royals and regular citizens. Since there are ethical rules regarding the destruction of tissue, which is necessary for genetic testing, the research team used body height, a highly hereditable characteristic, to look for evidence of incest.

"It is actually one of the largest collections of body height of ancient Egyptians and spans all major periods of their history."—Rühli.

The inbreeding among the pharaohs of Egypt was usually done to emulate the god Osiris, who married his sister Isis. Ramses II (c. 1303–1213 BC) married his own daughter Meritamen. He did have other wives, who were related in some way. Some married foreign royalty for political purposes to promote peace.

It was the women who carried the royal bloodlines so the men were wise to marry the most royal woman they could, often a close relative—hence a man was extremely fortunate to have a sister to marry. As a result, this inbreeding, consanguinity, was well-documented. According to *Smithsonian Magazine*, Egyptian law and tradition

"decreed that pharaohs marry their sisters. Cleopatra married her oldest brother after the death of her father, and she married her youngest brother after the death of her first brother."

The whole taboo of inbreeding came from the Romans—not the Greeks. Roman civil law forbade couples from marrying if they were within four degrees of consanguinity. From the mid-ninth century AD, the church even raised this limit to the seventh degree and the method of calculating degrees was also changed. Without question, incest in Egyptian culture was, in fact: (1) mimicking the Greek gods; and (2) among the wealthy, done to retain the wealth within the family.

Ptolemy II Philadelphos (308-246BC)
*pictured with Arsinoe II his second wife and sister
who had his first wife banished*

Ptolemy II Philadelphus (285–246 AD) ("brotherly love"), was the second ruler of the Ptolemaic Dynasty and the son of Ptolemy I and Berenice I, who died before 283 BC. He became joint ruler with his father two years before his death in 283 BC. Ptolemy II carried on his father's passion for expanding and building the Great Library of Alexandria. His construction efforts also included building the canal that linked the Nile to the Gulf of Suez.

Ptolemy II was married at first to Arsinoe I (282-247 BC), daughter of Lysimachus (c. 360–281 BC) of Thrace, in a political arrangement by his father to ensure peace and build support, about 288 BC. Arsinoe I was the mother of Ptolemy III (c. 280–222 BC). Their daughter, Berenike, was married to Antiochus II Theos of Syria (286–246 BC), also a political marriage to establish stability.

Ptolemy II has been known as *Philadelphus,* which was from the Greek, "Brotherly Love." When Philadelphia was founded by William Penn (1644–1718), a Quaker, it was on the principle of religious freedom. The first Catholic Church was erected there along with the first churches of just about every denomination. The whole slavery issue and the U.S. Civil War also involved religion. He named the city "Philadelphia," reading the Greek meaning of "brotherly love," yet not understanding the true story behind what it meant at that point in time. The "brotherly love" was not the Christian view of love thy brother, but incest. To suggest that Cleopatra was somehow Black is so farfetched, it is laughable.

Marcus Antonius (Mark Antony)
(83 - 30BC)
(Bust in the Vatican Museum)

Cleopatra VII
(51 - 30BC)

As I explained, the coinage of the era reflects the portraits of the various rulers, and they are highly accurate. We can see from the coinage and the bust of Mark Antony the depiction of his curly hair. A ruler would have to approve their portrait for production. The engravers had models of the person to work from. A collector can immediately recognize the person before reading the caption on the coinage.

We can easily see the resemblance between Cleopatra on her coinage to the surviving sculpture. She obviously did not have African features. This is a bronze tetradrachm depicting Cleopatra VII. We can more easily see how the portrait reflects the true image of Cleopatra.

Here is a coin from central Italy depicting an African and an elephant. Africans would often train elephants and then sell them to the Greek North Africans, such as the Carthaginians. It should be no surprise to find such a coin linking an African with an elephant from the interior of the continent. Elephants did not roam the northern regions of Africa.

Here is a coin from Ionia, modern Turkey. Here, too, we find a depiction of an African on early Greek coinage. While everyone asserts that the oldest profession is prostitution, the

ETRURIA, (Central Italy - Uncertain Mint)
Circa 300-250 BC Æ17mm (4.74 grams)
*Head of African right / Elephant standing right,
bell hanging from neck; below, pellet above Etruscan*

second-oldest is not lawyers to make sure the prostitutes get paid, but soldiers-for-hire. Indeed, the second oldest profession is most likely mercenaries. There were Black mercenaries who served in many wars. We know from contemporary accounts that the barbarians of the North were fearsome. These Celtic mercenaries were even hired by Egypt during the reign of the ethnically Greek Ptolemaic dynasty.

Celtic Mercenaries became a part of Egypt's official army. During the reign of Ptolemy III Euergetes (c. 280–222 BC), Celtic mercenaries played a very decisive role in conquering Syria as well as Judea. The Greek historian Polybius tells us that many Celtic mercenaries actually settled in Egypt and took Egyptian or Greek wives. The

IONIA, Phokaia. Circa 625/0-522 BC
*EL Hekte – Sixth Stater (10mm, 2.58 g). Head of African left,
wearing necklace; to right, seal downward / Rough incuse square.*

Greeks saw them as a mixed race and referred to their offspring as *e pigovoi*. There was no way Cleopatra was anything but Greek.

We also know from the historian Herodotus (c. 484-425 BC) that he visited Egypt during the fifth century BC. He made it clear that the Greeks were one of the first groups of foreigners that ever lived there. This Egyptian painting shows white and brown races. It is amazing that people would distort history to insist that Cleopatra was Black when the Ptolemy line was Greek, and they certainly did not intermarry with the locals regardless of their color.

Cleopatra VII
(51 - 30BC)
Æ Drachm of Egypt (16.84 grams)

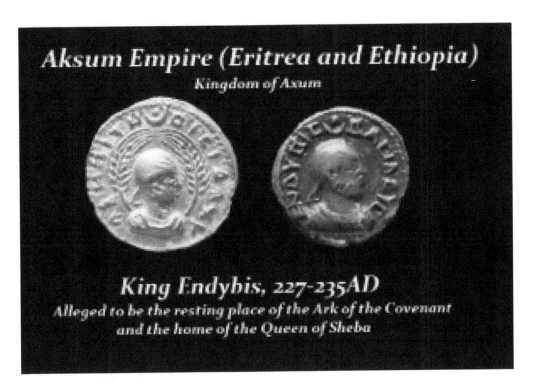

There were clearly black empires inside Africa. Endybis (227-235 AD) was a late-third-century sovereign of the Kingdom of Aksum in East Africa (modern-day Ethiopia and Eritrea). He was among the earliest rulers in the Horn of Africa to mint his own coins. The Aksumite currency of his reign was issued in gold and silver denominations and bore inscriptions in the Hellenistic Greek of Alexander the Great era.

The coins of Endybis are dated to c. 295 AD to c. 310 AD and were the oldest Aksumite coins. The portrait of Endybis is flanked by wheat, implying that their trade was grain, which was the source of the great wealth.

These gold coins are not particularly rare, implying that the empire was highly profitable in trade. There is little doubt that these Aksumite coins are closely linked with developments in the Roman empire during the third century.

Unlike India, which merely imitated Roman coins, here the currency reforms took place during the reign of Diocletian (284-305 AD) after the Great Monetary Collapse between 260 and 268 AD, implying that Endybis's coins appeared after the reforms of 294 AD. Because of the turmoil of this period in history, many of these coins have survived due to people hoarding their wealth and burying their coins for safekeeping.

This obsession to rewrite history attributing North Africa to Africans from the interior is a serious distortion of history. The Greeks colonized Northern Africa for centuries before Alexander showed up and conquered Egypt in 332 BC. Even the legendary Queen of Sheba was from Ethiopia, which depicted people of the Black race as distinguished from the white Jewish race. This whole wokeism today is going way too far as Netflix aired a show with Cleopatra being Black. What is next? Julius Caesar was really transgender?

Before the Greeks and Romans, there were the Phoenicians, who ruled the Mediterranean. The core of Phoenician territory was the city-state of Tyre in what-is-now Lebanon. Phoenicia was an ancient Semitic civilization originating in the Levant region of the eastern Mediterranean. The Phoenician civilization lasted from approximately 1550 to 300 BC, when the Persians, and later the Greeks, conquered Tyre. Phoenicians, along with the Jews and the Egyptians, were not a Black African race.

Hannibal
(c 247 – 183/181BC)

The Carthaginians were Phoenician settlers, not African from the interior, originating in the Mediterranean coast of the Near East. They spoke Canaanite, a Semitic language, and followed a local variety of the ancient Canaanite religion, the Punic religion. In fact, Carthage was a city founded by the Phoenicians. There is also no mention that Hannibal (247-181 BC) was African. Since coinage began among the Greek city-states, the Greeks became an inspiration for the Carthaginians, as was the case for the Romans. Many Greek deities were also integrated within the already-diverse Punic pantheon (the civilization of Carthage).

Phoenician merchants bartered, and being avid traders, it is surprising that they were not among the first to adopt the metal currency. It was only when they were conquered by the Persian king Darius I (c. 550–486 BC) becoming the fifth satrapy, which includes Syria, Palestine, and Cyprus, that we begin to see Phoenician coinage about 480 BC.

PHOENICIA, Sidon (Sakton) II
(Circa 401-365 BC)
AR Dishekel (27.24 grams)
Phoenician galley left waves below /
King of Persia and driver in chariot
King of Sidon standing left, in Egyptian dress

The life of Pythagoras (c. 570– 495 BC), who was regarded as a philosopher rather than a mathematician in ancient times, is obscured by legends. According to one tradition, he studied in Phoenicia first, then realizing that the lore of the Phoenicians was of Egyptian origin, he went to Egypt. He visited the priests of Heliopolis, Memphis, and Thebes and he was even said to have mastered the Egyptian language.[2]

Plato (424/423–348/347 BC) in Timaeus laid out an elaborately designed account of the formation of the universe and an explanation of its impressive order and beauty. Plato argued that the universe is the product of rational, purposive, and beneficent creation. This is also where he relayed the story of Atlantis. He explained that an Egyptian priest in Sais, the political and cultural center of Egypt during the XX Vl Dynasty, was the source of this story. The Egyptians made no claim of having an origin in Africa.

When Julius Caesar (100-44 BC) showed up, Cleopatra VII was in the midst of a power struggle with her husband/brother the younger Ptolemy XIV (c. 59–44 BC), who was restored to the throne after Ptolemy XIII (c. 62–47 BC) drowned in the Nile. It was the historian Plutarch (c. 46–119 AD) who described that she had her slave smuggle her into the palace bundled in an oversized sack to meet Caesar in the autumn of 48 BC. Cleopatra VII was petite, standing about five feet tall, which allowed her slave to easily smuggle her into the palace.

She was slender with an hourglass shape. Her skin was as white "as alabaster," which matched her hair, which was said to be light, tending to blondish-red. She had stunning green eyes, often called olive-toned eyes.

Plutarch tells us that she knew the ways of a woman to manipulate men. Her voice was said to be "like music" when she would speak. She was highly educated, spoke five languages, and was "dazzlingly intelligent." She knew very well her place in the history of the Greek Hellenistic world.

---

2   Diogenes Laertius, VIII.3 (Pythagoras).

Plutarch informs us: *"It was by this device of Cleopatra's, it is said, that Caesar was first captivated, for she showed herself to be a bold coquette"* (Life of Julius Caesar, XLIX.3). And it was there that her husband/brother, the young Ptolemy XIII, found them early the next morning in bed; Caesar had already been seduced by Cleopatra. She was also very fertile. Nine months later, her son Caesarion was born.

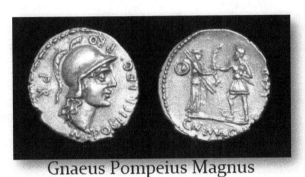

Gnaeus Pompeius Magnus
(ca. 75–April 12th, 45 BC)

ArmstrongEconomics.COM

Yet, Plutarch informs us that Caesar was not her first Roman manipulated. In a passing comment without elaboration, he reports that she used "her beauty upon Gaius Caesar and Gnaeus the son of Pompey" before Mark Antony. Plutarch adds: *"For Caesar and Pompey had known her when she was still a girl and inexperienced in affairs."* (Life of Antony, XXV.3–4).

The year before Cleopatra met Caesar, he had defeated Gnaeus Pompey (75-45 BC) at the Battle of Munda on March 17, 45 BC. Gnaeus and his brother Sextus managed to escape. Caesar had won the Civil War. Within a few weeks, Gnaeus Pompey was hunted down and killed by Lucius Caesennius Lento on April 12, 45 BC.

Cleopatra VII holding Ptolemy XV Caesarion
Struck at Cyprus, where an important temple to Aphodite was located at Paphos. In 48 BC, Julius Caesar gave Cyprus to Cleopatra, holding his son Caesarion

Cleopatra VII was smart and cunning. She sought to use her sex to entrap political elites such as Julius Caesar (100-44 BC) and bore his son with the hopes that the Ptolemy line would then rule Rome. Here is a coin she issued in Cyprus after Caesar gave her that territory showing her holding Caesar's son Caesarion. She had managed to get Caesar to give her Cyprus, expanding her own territory and demonstrating her thirst to restore the glory of the Greek world.

To seal a bond between Antony and Octavian, Mark Antony married Octavian's sister Octavia

(c. 66–11 BC) after his third wife, Fulvia, died. It took a senatorial decree to seal that marriage in 40

BC because Octavia was pregnant with her first husband's child. This was following Antony meeting Cleopatra in 41 BC.

Mark Antony & Octavia - Fleet Coinage AE As (8.56 grams) RPC1465

ArmstrongEconomics.COM

In 40 BC, Mark Antony and Octavian entered into the Treaty of Brundisium, whereby the eastern half of the Roman empire was assigned to Mark Antony. The fleet coinage was a set of bronze denominations issued to serve as small change for the region under his control, bringing Roman denominations to the region. Modern scholars have referred to this series of coinage as the "fleet coinage" because they were minted by three of Antony's fleet prefects. They issued six denominations all struck in bronze. The portrait shows Antony with his wife Octavia.

The fleet coinage was minted by Mark Antony in the eastern Mediterranean from 40 BC until his death in 30 BC. The bronze coinage is typically highly worn. It was an effort to introduce Roman denominations in the East, which had always retained the Greek monetary system even after their conquest by Rome. That they bare the portraits of Mark Antony and Octavia was clearly a political alliance.

Gaius Cassius Longinus
(c. 86 BC – October 3rd, 42 BC)

ArmstrongEconomics.COM

When Caesar was assassinated, Cleopatra showed just how cunning she really was. There were allegations that surfaced about how Cleopatra had been raising money for Cassius (86-42 BC), who was one of the assassins of Caesar against the Second Triumvirate led by Octavian. Cassius was the brother-in-law of Marcus Junius Brutus (c. 85–42 BC), the most famous of Caesar's assassins. After the assassination, Brutus and the others fled Rome and ran off to Asia. They were funded in part by the Persians.

Cassius (42BC) Fourrée Denarius (20mm, 2.23 grams)

We do know that Cleopatra received messages requesting military aid from both Cassius and Publius Cornelius Dolabella, who was proconsul of Syria. She appears to have decided to write to Cassius, claiming

Alexander III the Great
(356-323BC)

that her kingdom faced too many internal problems to fund his war. However, she sent the four legions left by Caesar in Egypt to Dolabella. The coins confirm that there was a shortage of money because there are Fourrée[3] denarii of Brutus and Cassius that appear to have been struck from genuine dies, suggesting they were creating forgeries of their own coins to fund the war.

Cassius managed to capture these legions in Palestine on their way to Syria. However, it was Cleopatra's governor of Cyprus, Serapion, who defected to Cassius, providing him with Egyptian ships. This was probably the origin of the allegation that Cleopatra was funding the assassins against Octavian and Antony. Cleopatra then took her own fleet to Greece, insisting that she intended to personally assist Octavian and Antony. Curiously, she claimed there was a storm, which delayed her arrival and caused her to be too late to aid in the battle. Thus, she had all sides covered. We can see, Cleopatra was cunning and had the end objective of conquering Rome to reestablish the empire of Alexander the Great.

This has always created a cloud over the facts. Why would Cleopatra aid the assassins? Perhaps she was intuitive. She knew that Octavian was Caesar's heir and as such her son was a threat to Octavian. Hence, Cassius may have assassinated Caesar, but Octavian was her threat now and would kill her son.

As part of her scheme to elevate her connection to Caesar, she conceived the idea of establishing what was known as the Caesareum of Alexandria—the ancient temple in Alexandria, Egypt, dedicated to Julius Caesar.

Cleopatra commissioned a sculpture of Julius Caesar carved in black basalt. The image above depicts the black basalt bust of Caesar which was an Egyptian stone reserved for people of the highest rank. This may have been the only bust that was there. We know that the Caesareum stood opposite the harbor of Alexandria.

Cleopatra's construction of the Caesareum in honor of Julius Caesar was a major political

Brutus, 42 BC Silver Denarius
"EIDMAR" Declaring He Killed Caesar
on the Ides of March
ArmstrongEconomics.COM

---

3   Fourrée meaning stuffed–copper core with thin sheet of silver applied during striking.

maneuver. She also had his son, Caesarion, so this decision was clearly to show support for Caesar's only male heir.

Ptolemy XIV died in 44 BC, and Cleopatra's co-ruler became her own infant son, Ptolemy XV Caesar (47–30 BC), who was born June 23, 47 BC. He was about seventeen years old when his mother was confronted in 30 BC by Octavian. He is often known being the son of Caesar as Caesarion. Here is his image with his mother on the wall at the Temple of Hathor. Indeed, she was correct. Octavian needed to eliminate Caesarion. His friend, Arius Didymus, was said to have warned him: "Too many Caesars is not good."

However, there was some controversy that Caesarion was not really fathered by Caesar. He was said to have looked like Caesar; yet it has been argued that Caesar himself had not officially acknowledged him as his son. Gaius Oppius managed much of Caesar's private affairs, and he was said to have considerable influence in Rome during Caesar's absence.

It is Suetonius (Caesar, 56), who even suggested that Oppius wrote the histories of the Spanish, African, and Alexandrian wars that were published as the works of Caesar. Oppius also wrote a life of Caesar and the elder Scipio. This is where it gets interesting. Following Caesar's death, Oppius apparently wrote a pamphlet attempting to prove that Caesarion, Cleopatra's son, was not actually fathered by Caesar as she claimed. We cannot dismiss the fact that he may have been bribed or simply personally motivated to cast doubt on Caesarion in favor of Octavia. This added to the contest between Octavian and his rivals—Antony and Cleopatra.

The Meeting Of Antony And Cleopatra
By Lawrence Alma-Tadema (1836–1912)

It was after the Battle of Philippi, in October 42 BC in Macedonia, where Brutus and Cassius were defeated. Octavian returned to Rome, while Antony remained in Tarsus in Asia Minor where he planned to carry out Caesar's original intention to invade Parthia for also funding Brutus. In 41 BC, while still in Tarsus, Mark Antony summoned Cleopatra VII, now Queen of Egypt, former lover of Caesar, to answer reports that she had aided his enemies, lending money to Cassius in particular.

Plutarch tells us that he sent Dellius to deliver the order. However, when Dellius . . .

"saw how Cleopatra looked, and noticed her subtlety and cleverness in conversation, at once perceived that Antony would not so much as think of doing such a woman any harm, but that she would have the greatest influence with him. He therefore resorted to flattery and tried to induce the Egyptian to go to Cilicia "decked out in fine array" (as Homer would say), and not to be afraid of Antony, who was the most agreeable and humane of commanders. She was persuaded by Dellius, and judging by the proofs which she had had before this of the effect of her beauty upon Caius Caesar and Gnaeus the son of Pompey, she had hopes that she would more easily bring Antony to her feet."

Cleopatra was about twenty-one years old when she met Mark Antony. Seven years later, in 41 BC, she met Antony again at Tarsus on the river Cydnus. She was now nearly thirty years old and confident that she could allay the suspicions that she had funded Cassius against Antony and Octavian. Mark Antony became her third Roman target. Plutarch informs us:

"she had hopes that she would more easily bring Antony to her feet . . . she was going to visit Antony at the very time when women have the most brilliant beauty and are at the acme of intellectual power. Therefore . . . she went putting her greatest confidence in herself, and in the charms and sorceries of her own person." (Life of Antony, XXV.3–4)

Cleopatra visited Antony and seduced him. Being fertile, it was then that she conceived, and later gave birth to twins. She was beautiful, but more than that, she was brilliant and cunning. Plutarch further explains:

"For her beauty, as we are told, was in itself not altogether incomparable, nor such as to strike those who saw her; but converse with her had an irresistible charm, and her presence, combined with the persuasiveness of her discourse and the character which was somehow diffused about her behavior towards others, had something stimulating about it. There was sweetness also in the tones of her voice; and her tongue, like an instrument of many strings, she could readily turn to whatever language she pleased." (XXVII.2-3)

Most have focused only on her beauty—for to have Shakespeare write a play about you, to sell it, he had to spin it into a great love affair at first sight. Yet Plutarch remarks that the Romans pitied Antony for having pushed aside Octavia for Cleopatra *"especially those who had seen Cleopatra and knew that neither in youthfulness nor beauty was she superior to Octavia."* (LVII.3)

It was certainly not the often-claimed issue of Antony dumping Octavia the older woman for the younger Cleopatra since they were both the same age. All this attention to her beauty and others desperately trying to convert her to an African, gloss over the fact that she was exceptionally intelligent and cunning. This was not sexual or a love fling. It was a calculated use of her charms and beauty to conquer Rome and restore the greatness of the Greeks and the empire that was forged by Alexander the Great.

Cleopatra VII
(69-30BC)
Vatican Museum

Cleopatra was well-educated and nostalgic about her Greek heritage. She saw herself as an heir of Alexander the Great, whose tomb was also in Alexandria. She was clearly seeking to take over the Roman Empire, as her vision of a descendant of Macedonia and the Empire of Alexander the Great. We do know that Julius Caesar visited Alexander's tomb out of respect. However, it has been lost and may have been destroyed by the Christians during the fourth or fifth centuries AD under the false assumption that it was a monument to a pagan god.

Following Caesar's assassination, Cleopatra needed a plan B. Perhaps she funded Cassius out of fear of Octavian. The defect of her governor of Cyprus was a perfect political cover. This is standard, just as Biden blew up Nord Stream pipeline and tried to blame it on Putin. Perhaps when summoned by Antony, she then turned her sights on Antony to seduce him as well and to turn him against Octavian to protect her son and his claim to Rome. She was clever and understood how to use her womanly attributes to twist men around her little finger. But above all, she was certainly no fool.

Being summoned by Marc Antony, understanding the allegations, Cleopatra did what she had to do—seduce Antony. Apparently, that is when, being quite fertile, she conceived and bore him twins thereby sealing their destiny together.

Egyptian statue announcing Cleopatra & Mark Antony's twins
Cleopatra Selene and Alexander Helios

Cleopatra's relationship with Antony was simply the equivalent of a dynastic marriage. Therefore, giving birth to twins was not seen as anything but a dynastic relationship to secure the power of Egypt, as in her prior relationship with Caesar. The telltale sign that Cleopatra was seeking to restore the Macedonian kingdom of Alexander the Great was revealed in the naming of her children. All three children—Cleopatra Selene, Alexander Helios, and Ptolemy XV Caesar (Caesarion) —had their names very carefully selected. They had Macedonian and Ptolemaic precedents linking them to the royal house of Alexander the Great. The twin's second names, Helios (Sun) and Selene (Moon), associated them with prophecies that Rome was to enter a new golden age. That was coming from astrology, but it turned out to be the new imperial age for Rome—not Cleopatra.

Cleopatra certainly believed in this prophecy of the coming of a golden age. She turned Antony against Octavian to create her proxy war just as the United States neocons used Ukraine to instigate their war against Russia. In both instances, they believed that they would usher in a new golden age. The defeat of Octavian and Caesarion taking the throne of Rome would mean that Macedonia would rise again.

There was no whirlwind love affair of popular romantic fiction. Plutarch started that vision by writing that Antony needed Cleopatra physically and emotionally. Cleopatra was simply not head-over-heels in love with Mark Antony, nor was she some prostitute. She was engaging in a calculated maneuver to manipulate Antony for her political gain to reestablish the Macedonian Empire. This is what jumps out at you from a review of her coinage.

It took Cleopatra some time to sway Mark Antony. She was simply his mistress and was using sex to create a hold over him in addition to bearing him twins. Despite Antony's marriage to Octavia, Cleopatra bore him three children, which further strained Antony's relations with Octavian. He eventually divorced Octavia in 33 BC and that severed the bond. Antony attempted to not only recognize the children as his, but he tried to set them up with ownership of lands from his conquests in the east, including Egypt, Syria, Armenia, and much of Anatolia (modern-day Turkey).

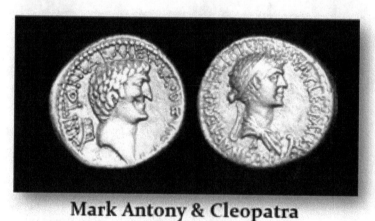

Mark Antony & Cleopatra
perhaps the finest know surviving Roman silver denarius
ArmstrongEconomics.COM

The issue of this Roman denarius with her portrait was certainly struck in Alexandria, not Rome. The legends and iconography clearly connect them to Antony's campaign against Armenia in 34 BC and the subsequent infamous 'Donations of Alexandria.' Look closely; at the lower right of Cleopatra is the prow of a ship, while behind the head of Mark Antony is the Armenian tiara of the former king.

Upon Antony's return from what was little more than a looting expedition to distract from his disastrous defeats against the Parthians (Persians), a great victory spectacle was organized in the Egyptian capital—not Rome.

Mark Antony
AR Denarius (bare hd rt/Tiara on bow & arrow)
CR 539/1

This denarius issued by Antony displays the Armenian tiara. Captives were paraded and donatives distributed. Most striking, however, was that the queen and Antony distributed titles and kingdoms to themselves and their children, with Cleopatra being named "Queen of Kings" and "Queen of Egypt." She claimed Cyprus, which had been a gift from Caesar. She also claimed Libya and central Syria for herself. Alexander Helios received Armenia, Media, and Parthia, while his twin sister, Cleopatra Selene, received Cyrenaica and Libya, and Ptolemy Syria, Phoenicia, and Cilicia.

Halley's Comet has been recorded as early as 467 BC by the Greeks. Tigranes II the Great (95-56 BC) of Armenia issued the earliest coin depicting Halley's Comet, represented by the star in his tiara. This was the kingdom which Antony looted, for it had no meaningful means of defense against Antony.

**Kingdom of Armenia, Tigranes II the Great
(95-56 BC)**
AR Tetradrachm Draped bust right,
wearing Armenian tiara with five peaks & Haley's Comet

Mark Antony and Cleopatra VII
(83-30BC)   (69-30BC)
AR Silver Tetradrachm (11.12 grams)
ArmstrongEconomics.COM

These donations of what were, except for Egypt proper, mostly either Roman provinces or unconquered lands (such as Media and Parthia), caused great outrage in Roman society. Worst of all was the proclamation of Julius Caesar's and Cleopatra's mutual son, Caesarion, as King of Kings, god, and *divi filius* ('son of god'), and Antony's appointment as Caesar's sole legitimate heir. This clearly fell into the scheme of Cleopatra, who was seeking to reestablish the empire of Alexander the Great. As I have said, she was cunning, and highly intelligent.

This was a direct challenge to Octavian's claim to power, which stemmed from his adoption by Julius Caesar and the loyalty of the Caesar's legions. This would only accelerate the irreversible break between Antony and Octavian—the most powerful men of the Roman world cleverly being manipulated by Cleopatra.

This allocation of territory to the children of Cleopatra was resented by the Romans and helped erode much of Antony's support with the public and the Senate. Octavian knew that the people still loved Antony and he needed to somehow win universal support. He needed to manipulate the Senate into stripping Antony of all power.

While both Antony and Octavian were soliciting the senators to support their cause, there was deep concern about Cleopatra and her motives. Octavian capitalized on the situation by reading a copy of Antony's will which gave much of his control to Cleopatra's children. Regardless of the authenticity of the will, the propaganda worked, and the Senate declared war on Cleopatra and, thus, indirectly on Antony as well. Caesarion, the son of Cleopatra and Caesar, was clearly a major threat to Octavian.

Octavian was indeed very clever. He suggested that Antony was not himself and that the entire plot was indeed Cleopatra and her thirst to take control of Rome. This was her proxy war to conquer the Roman Empire and reestablish the Empire of Alexander the Great.

Octavian's base of power was his link with Caesar through adoption. Caesarion was a serious threat to this loyalty of the legions. Antony had declared that Caesarion was the legitimate heir to Julius Caesar, at the clever behest of Cleopatra. This became a propaganda war for the future of the Roman Empire. Cleopatra instigated her proxy war to conquer Rome. The Second Triumvirate ended on the last day of 33 BC.

Agrippa
AR Drachm of Masicytus, Lycia (27-20BC)
Bare head of Agrippa right; Λ-Y across fields / Two citharas; MA below
ArmstrongEconomics.COM

Finally, the Senate deprived Antony of his power and declared war against Cleopatra. A third of the Senate and both consuls joined Antony's side. In 31 BC, the war began when Octavian's talented general Marcus Agrippa (63 BC-12 AD) captured the Greek city and naval port of Methone, which was loyal to Antony. Mark Antony was an excellent soldier, but his lack of experience in naval engagements was to be his downfall.

Mark Antony, (struck 44-30 BC)
AR Denarius with M. Junius Silanus, quaestor pro consule
Military mint moving with Antony, probably Athens, summer 32BC
Crawford 542/1
ArmstrongEconomics.COM

This coin of Mark Antony was struck by M. Junius Silanus, illustrating the perils of the period. During the civil war that now erupted between Octavian and Mark Antony, choosing sides could be a life-or-death decision. The career of Silanus illustrates a challenge that all subordinate Roman politicians faced during the crisis. Silanus obviously followed the course of the wars. Siding with none of the imperatorial figures was a wise choice to avoid this life-or-death decision. Loyal supporters of fallen generals risked facing execution, while early defectors were usually pardoned and allowed to continue their careers.

Silanus first served under Lepidus before supporting Mark Antony in 43 BC in the Battle of Mutina. Later he sided with Sextus Pompey and was pardoned in 39 BC. He served as quaestor pro consul of Antony in 33-32 BC. He defected to Octavian on the eve of the Battle of Actium in 31 BC. He was then rewarded and became consul in 25 BC. This coin was struck in Athens in the summer of 32 BC, when the forces of Mark Antony were gathering in Greece for the final clash against Octavian in the Battler of Actium. These were challenging times for everyone. You had to choose your allegiances very carefully.

Antony's generals certainly did not trust Cleopatra or her armies. This effectively undermined Antony's position. Octavian used the question of Cleopatra as his main propaganda strategy that Antony's legions were subservient to Cleopatra.

Antony's generals were aware of Octavian's propaganda to undermine the morale of their legions. This was the very reason WHY Antony produced his legionary denarii—to counter that propaganda and claim that he had overwhelming support.

Antony's generals concluded that Cleopatra's presence was the very source of Octavian's propaganda. They argued that Cleopatra should return to Egypt. They tried to persuade her that many within the Roman Senate, the Roman people, and the Roman army itself would abandon their support of Octavian if she left and returned to Egypt. That was precisely against her agenda and why she was funding the war to begin with.

The worst contribution of Cleopatra was her military advice to Antony. Where Antony's generals were much more experienced with land battles, it was Cleopatra who insisted that Antony had the advantage on the water and should attack by sea since that was Egyptian experience. Interestingly, Cleopatra did not trust turning her control over to Antony unless she was present and thus refused to leave. Antony took Cleopatra's advice to his detriment.

Mark Antony is said to have possessed 500 ships. If the coinage was valid, his total force would have been about 182,000 men. Other sources claim that Antony had an infantry force of 70,000. Octavian had 400 ships and 80,000 infantry who were stationed at Corinth.

Agrippa Æ As (29mm, 12.78 grams) Rome Mint
Struck under Caligula RIC I 58 (Gaius)

ArmstrongEconomics.COM

Agrippa brilliantly managed to trap portions of Antony's army, both on land and sea. They deserted and fled to Octavian's side upon realizing they were really fighting for Cleopatra. The morale of Antony's legions had been successfully undermined by Octavian's propaganda focusing on Cleopatra. They had followed Antony for he had been the right hand of Caesar unlike the boyish Octavian who was viewed as an upstart.

Roman Quinquereme

However, some reported that in the middle of the night before battle, Antony lost some 19 infantry legions and 12,000 cavalry before there was ever a chance for a battle on land.

Antony's fleet was made up of primarily large ships known as *quinqueremes* that were covered in bronze plates. Octavianus' fleet was made up of the smaller Liburnian vessels that were faster and much more maneuverable. The quinqueremes had the strategic advantage of height from which to shoot into an opponent's vessel. The bronze plates were used to protect them from ramming, which was the main objective in a naval battle to sink the other's ship.

Antony's quinqueremes could not maneuver fast enough to even ram the smaller, more agile ships of Octavian. Ironically, the smaller Liburnian ships lacked the strength of structure to do much damage even if they did ram the plated quinqueremes. This was likely the reason why Antony listened to Cleopatra.

According to our most detailed accounts, Antony's largest warships were undermanned and, as a result, were unable to

Liburnian Ship

execute the tactics for which they were designed—powerful, head-on collisions. This tended to support what I had long suspected, that Antony's legionary coinage was propaganda to try to convince Octavian and the Senate that he had overwhelming support.

Battle of Actium

Marcus Agrippa was one of the best military generals at the time. Agrippa succeeded in pulling off a strategic move to cut Antony's lines of communication further down the coast. This unleashed disunity within Antony's legions and disrupted coordination among his generals and Cleopatra.

Consequently, Antony rowed out in two wings to attack Octavian's fleet, which had gathered at the entrance to the gulf in their blockade. Antony tried to flank Octavian's right but that exposed his own center. When Agrippa saw the center exposed, he moved to exploit it, creating confusion as the fighting then grew extensive. Cleopatra and her squadron of sixty ships suddenly raised their sails and raced away from the center of the battle to the open ocean.

Roman Slingshot Bullet Stone

Excavations have uncovered large catapult stones. While Antony's ships were meant for ramming, Agrippa kept his distance and filled the sky with catapult stones and fire in addition to arrows and slingshot stone bullets as we have here.

When Antony's plan had clearly failed, yet in the midst of the intense fighting, Cleopatra led the rearguard squadron of sixty ships through the center of the melee and hoisted sail to flee south. Her move precipitated a general flight, but the bulk of Antony's fleet was unable to disengage from their opponents.

Antony himself transferred his flag to a smaller vessel and successfully slipped past Octavian's line. The remainder of the fleet was not so fortunate and was abandoned to an enemy intent upon its destruction with fire projectiles.

For centuries, historians have been baffled by Antony's reaction of fleeing the Battle of Actium on September 2, 31 BC once he saw Cleopatra leaving. Antony abandoned the command ship and followed her with forty ships of his own. Many saw this as a lovesick fool confused when his lover decided to leave him. Others have proposed that he knew the battle was lost and he planned to flee with Cleopatra once her ships had the opportunity to break free. What is clear is that Antony abandoned the bulk of his fleet in the middle of the battle, leaving the remainder to their fate. Once Antony's legions realized he had dishonorably abandoned them, they surrendered to Agrippa.

It was during this collapse in order that sheer chaos unfolded. This was, as typical in war, when the greatest number of casualties were sustained. One writer describes the battle's end as a great burning of Antony's ships; another says the sea was so choked with royal wreckage that the water was flecked with purple and gold. The destruction was complete. From Antony's original fleet of 500 warships, only a few more than sixty returned to Egypt.

A myth of antiquity that was invoked by Pliny the Elder to explain the defeat of Antony and Cleopatra against Octavian at the naval battle of Actium involved a fish, called *echeneis,* or *remora.* It was believed that this fish had the power to stop ships, or to delay their motion by adhering to the hull. Antony's fleet was immobile and could not thrust forward to ram Octavian's ships. Antony's fleet was unable to use the ramming tactics because the wave resistance was increased up to ten times compared to the Octavian fleet and could not advance.

Battle Actium by Johann Georg Platzer (1704–1761)

The Battle of Actium was perhaps one of the most important battles in history. Yes, it marked the defeat of Mark Antony and Cleopatra, ending the line of the Ptolemy Dynasty and thus the remanent of the Empire of Alexander the Great. Yet, it was also the end of the Roman Republic, giving birth to the emergence of Imperial Rome. It was Octavian's victory that saved Rome from Cleopatra and resulted in the Roman Senate bestowing upon him the title of Augustus—meaning first among citizens, or venerable.

The Battle of Actium ended the thirteen-year-long rivalry between Octavian and Antony following the assassination of Julius Caesar on March 15, 44 BC. Cleopatra's manipulation of Antony, including his divorce from Octavia and granting of territories to her children, was all part of one act to divide Antony and Octavian, and then fund a proxy civil war for the overthrow of the Roman Empire. Cleopatra was playing a game of very high-stakes poker.

Following the Battle of Actium, the defeated Antony sent a message to Scarpus, urging him to join him with his four legions in Alexandria to continue the fight. Scarpus, however, had the envoy executed and sent word to Octavian that he would join his cause, while striking coins with an open hand as a gesture of peace towards Caesar's triumphant adoptive son. Octavian graciously accepted Scarpus's defection from Antony, leaving him in office until at least 27 BC. Obviously, Octavian was also engaging in propaganda with no intention of offering peace to Cleopatra and Caesarion.

With Cleopatra sensing defeat, fleeing the battle early and Antony abandoning his own troops to follow her to Alexandria, everything changed. Octavian then pressed onward to Alexandria, aided by Scarpus's defection. He finally arrived after almost a year's slow journey.

Octavian
Denarius celebrating the victory at Actium
Trophy denoting the naval battle with a prow of a ship
Roman Imperial Coins 265a
ArmstrongEconomics.COM

Mark Antony   Octavian

Octavian (44-27 BC)
AR Denarius by Pinarius Scarpus, moneyer
Open Right hand to left/Victory on globe, holding wreath
Crawford 546/6
ArmstrongEconomics.COM

The Flight to Egypt

Cleopatra

Octavian/Augustus

CLEOPATRA TRIED ONCE again to use her charms on Octavian, but they had no effect. Cleopatra could neither charm nor negotiate her way out of this situation. Cassio Dio tells us that Cleopatra and Antony tried to arouse the enthusiasm of the Egyptians as Octavian would surely turn to Egypt.

Antony and Cleopatra were making their preparations for war both on land and by sea. They were calling all the neighboring tribes and the kings who had once supported them. They were planning to sail to Spain to stir up a revolt using the wealth of Egypt. They were also planning to set up a base of operations in the Red Sea. Cassio Dio even mentions that Cleopatra hoped that she could kill Octavian by some means of treachery.

Cleopatra dispatched emissaries carrying peace proposals to Octavian and even offered monetary bribes to his followers. The true nature of Cleopatra emerged; she simply used Antony for her goal to conquer Rome and restore the glory of Macedonia and the Empire of Alexander the Great. Cleopatra did not tell Antony that she had sent Octavian a golden scepter and a golden crown with the royal throne, signifying through them that she offered him the kingdom as well.

Octavian (44 - 27BC)
AR Denarius (18mm, 3.61 grams) Military Mint
Traveling with Octavian in Cisalpine Gaul April-July 43 BC
Bare head right / Equestrian statue of Octavian left
The first appearance of Octavian's portrait

ArmstrongEconomics.COM

Octavian accepted her gifts as a good omen. However, he did not answer with any respect to Antony and his fate. Octavian's response was public that Cleopatra had to give up her armed forces and renounce even her sovereignty over Egypt. Only then would Octavian consider what ought to be done in her case. Secretly, he also demanded that she must kill Antony. Only then would he grant her any pardon and leave her realm intact.

As Cleopatra was trying to negotiate with her once allies, the Arabians, instigated by Quintus Didius, the governor of Syria, burned the ships in the Arabian Gulf which had been built for the voyage to the Red Sea. He prevented any loyal troops of Cleopatra from returning to Egypt. Cassius Dio informs us that "the peoples and princes without exception refused their assistance to Antony." Everyone abandoned Antony after flight he followed Cleopatra and abandoned his army.

Cleopatra once again attempted to negotiate, this time promising Octavian vast amounts of precious metal. Antony tried to compromise, reminding Octavian of their friendship and kinship. Antony offered Publius Turullius, who was a senator and one of the assassins of Caesar and was living with Antony as a friend, if Octavian spared Cleopatra. Octavian gave no answer to Antony.

Antony dispatched a third embassy, sending him his son Antyllus with much gold. Octavian graciously accepted the money but sent the boy back once again, giving no reply. Cleopatra said she collected all the wealth of the Egyptian treasury and moved it to her tomb, threatening to burn it all up with her in case she should fail of even the slightest of her demands.

Octavian wanted the wealth of Egypt, which was said to be greater than any nation. Indeed, the sheer quantity of Antony's legionary denarii proved that point when it still accounted for up to 20% of the Roman money supply 100 years later.

This threat moved Octavian, who sent Thyrsus to make promises to Cleopatra, and even tried to claim he loved her too. Now he hoped that she would kill Antony and retain everything from her wealth to her throne.

Antony learned that Cornelius Gallus had taken over Scarpus's army and had suddenly marched with these troops upon Paraetonium and occupied it. Gallus laid chains underwater stretched at night across the mouth of the harbor. When his opposing ships entered the harbor, he raised the chains, trapping them and then burning them. With the news concerning Pelusium, Antony returned from Paraetonium.

He attempted to confront Caesar in front of Alexandria using his cavalry. Antony shot arrows into Caesar's camp carrying leaflets which promised the men six thousand sesterces. Octavian personally read the leaflets and played Cleopatra's quest to conquer Rome, suggesting this was treachery. He used this to boost morale against the Egyptian queen and Antony.

Antony took refuge in his fleet. Cleopatra was uncertain if he planned to battle or flee to Spain. Thus, she ordered the ships to desert Antony. It was said that she pretended to rush to her mausoleum, out of fear of Octavian preparing to take her life. She wanted Antony to know this, as it was an invitation for him to follow her. Cassius Dio reported that Antony had a suspicion that Cleopatra was betraying him. She had her servants inform Antony that she was dead so he would commit suicide. Her servants informed Antony that she was dead. When Antony heard this news, he knew his support was gone. There was no queen to fund any future war. He then committed suicide, not out of some lovesick passion, but from a practical viewpoint that all was lost.

Octavian & Mark Antony
Gold Aureus (8.08 grams)
Struck circa 39BC
Crawford 529/1
ArmstrongEconomics.COM

Cassius Dio tells us that Antony first asked one of the bystanders to slay him; but the man drew his sword and instead slew himself. Antony wished to *"imitate his courage and so gave himself a wound and fell upon his face, causing the bystanders to believe that he was dead. At this an outcry was raised, and Cleopatra, hearing it, peered out over the top of the tomb."*

Dedié a Son Altesse Imperiale Monseigneur   LA MORT DE MARC ANTOINE   Paul Petrowitz Grand Duc de toutes les Russies &c.

When Antony learned that Cleopatra was alive, Cassius Dio tells us that he stood up, but had lost much blood. He despaired and asked bystanders to carry him to the monument and to hoist him up by the ropes that were still there from the construction. Thus, Cassius Dio says that Antony died there in Cleopatra's arms.

Cleopatra now felt a certain confidence that Octavian would spare her. She sent word to Octavian that Antony was dead. She apparently remained there in her mausoleum. She hoped to buy her pardon and that of Egypt with her wealth but would never renounce her crown. She was the last of the Ptolemy rulers and always knew her place in history. As Dio explains, she preferred to *die with the name and dignity of a sovereign than to live in a private station.*

Cleopatra was prepared to set a fire to consume her wealth, if need be, and release poisonous asps that she had tested on servants to see in in what manner they died.

Octavian wanted to capture Cleopatra alive for a great triumph in Rome where she would be traditionally strangled at its conclusion. He also wanted the wealth of Egypt. Octavian intended to treat her as a captive. He did not want to make any false promises out of his own dignity. He sent Gaius Proculeius to obtain an audience with Cleopatra. He presented some moderate proposals but seized her before any agreement was reached.

Cleopatra VII (51 – 30BC)
Æ 80 drachmae, Alexandria (circa 50-40BC)(19.53 grams)
Diademed bust right/Rev. ΒΑΣΙΛΙΣΣΗΣ – ΚΛΕΟΠΑΤΡΑΣ
Eagle standing l. on thunderbolt

They removed any means by which she could cause her own death. She was allowed to spend some days during the embalming process of Antony's body. She was then removed to the palace and allowed her to retain attendants. This was to give her a false hope that she would retain her rank. Cleopatra asked to appear before Caesar and to have an interview with him. Octavian granted her request. To deceive her even more, he promised that he would come to her himself.

She prepared herself and gathered all the letters from Caesar to her. When Octavian entered, Cassius Dio tells us she stood and said:

"Hail, master—for Heaven has granted you the mastery and taken it from me. But surely you can see with your own eyes how your father looked when he visited me on many occasions, and you have heard people tell how he honored me in various ways and made me queen of the Egyptians. 3 That you may, however, earn something about me from him himself, take and read the letters which he wrote me with his own hand."

After much theater about her connection to Caesar and an attempt to employ her charm, Octavian pretended to be moved. He spoke: *"Be of good cheer, woman, and keep a stout heart; for you shall suffer no harm."* She noticed that he would not look her in the eye, and this greatly distressed her. He said nothing about her kingdom nor uttered a word of love for her to manipulate.

Cleopatra fell at his knees and said:

"I neither wish to live nor can I live, Caesar. But this favour I beg of you in memory of your father, that, since Heaven gave me to Antony after him, I may also die with Antony. 7 Would that I had

*perished then, straightway after Caesar! But since it was decreed by fate that I should suffer this affliction also,**11** send me to Antony; grudge me not burial with him, in order that, as it is because of him I die, so I may dwell with him even in Hades."*

Still, Octavian did not answer. Fearing that Cleopatra might commit suicide and ruin his triumph, he once again told her to be of good cheer. He wanted her to look spectacular for his triumph for the entire time he had claimed that she had subdued Pompey Jr., Caesar, and Antony with her looks.

Octavian left her with her attendants. Cleopatra apparently could read between the words. She suspected that she would be paraded as a trophy. This was, as Cassius Dio explained, a fate "worse than a thousand deaths." When she could accomplish nothing, she pretended to set great hopes in Octavian that he would achieve what he wanted. She said she would sail of her own free will to Rome. She prepared some treasured gifts to impress Octavian and relieve any fears she would commit suicide.

When Octavian's guards believed that Cleopatra would not commit suicide, they relaxed their watch over her, and she made her preparations to die as painlessly as possible. She prepared a will that was to be given to Octavian requesting that she be buried alongside Antony. She gave the sealed will to Octavian's man pretending that it contained some other matter. She was then free of his presence. Cleopatra then put on her most beautiful apparel, arranged her body in the appropriate fashion befitting her rank, and gathered all the emblems of royalty in her hands.

How she died is not known. The only marks on her body were slight pricks on the arm. That is where the story originated that she died from the bite of an asp concealed and smuggled to her. Cassius Dio tells us that others claimed Cleopatra had smeared a pin that she used to fasten her hair with poison. Previously, she had worn this pin in her hair as usual, but now she had made a slight scratch on her arm and had dipped the pin in the blood.

We are told that Octavian tried to resuscitate Cleopatra for his grand plans of displaying her in his triumph over Egypt would perhaps win him the status of dictator.

Archaeology

An Ancient Tunnel Discovered Beneath an Egyptian Temple May Lead to Cleopatra's Tomb, Archaeologists Say

For nearly 20 years, archaeologists have been searching the area around the temple Tapuziris Magna for the final resting place of the Egyptian queen and her husband Mark Antony.

Sarah Cascone, November 7, 2022

An alabaster statue of Cleopatra is shown to the press at the temple of Tasposiris Magna on the outskirts of Alexandria, on April 19, 2009. Archaeologists are now more convinced than ever that the tomb of Marc Anthony and Cleopatra lies nearby. Photo credit should read Cris Bouroncle/AFP via Getty Images.

The tomb of Antony and Cleopatra is the undiscovered burial crypt of Mark Antony and Cleopatra VII from 30 BC. It is assumed to be located near ancient Alexandria, Egypt. According to historians Suetonius and Plutarch, the Roman leader Octavian permitted their burial together after he had defeated them, at least honoring Cleopatra's dying request. Archaeologists have discovered a rock-cut tunnel beneath Egypt's ancient Taposiris Magna Temple. They are hopeful that it may lead to the lost tomb of Cleopatra and Mark Antony, who were embalmed together in the same tomb as by Egyptian custom.

The portrayal of Cleopatra and Antony being in a genuine love affair appears to be the age-old desire to create love stories of ever after. She was not bumbling from one lover to the next. She knew her place in the history and majesty of Alexander the Great. As Cassius Dio pointed out, to be hauled off to Rome and displayed as a trophy of Octavian was a fate worse than a thousand deaths. This is the pride of her station in history, not the fear of a lovesick woman.

The machinations of this very clever queen always pointed to her end goal: the conquest of Rome for the glory of Macedonia. She used Julius Caesar to gain sole power in Egypt. She was certainly not shy nor subservient to her younger brother and his handlers who sought control over him and clearly understood that Cleopatra was neither a fool nor passive.

Caesar's time with Cleopatra resulted in a son, Ptolemy XV Caesarion. That was certainly a major playing card in this game for power. Was he really Caesar's? That we will never know. But she did appear to be quite fertile.

Gaius Suetonius Tranquillus (c. 69–122 AD) and Appian of Alexandria (c. 95–165 AD) both mention that Caesar's time with Cleopatra was brief. It was not a whirlwind romance; it may have lasted less than forty days. Appian even goes further and states that "[Caesar] in company with Cleopatra and enjoying himself with her in other ways" (*The Civil Wars*, II.90) and tried to get him to stay longer in Egypt. Certainly, Cleopatra visited Rome in 46 BC with Ptolemy XIV, who was honored by Caesar, suggesting he was not inclined to abandon everything for her. She was hosted in Caesar's villa and deified with statuary at the temple of Venus Genetrix. Cleopatra was also in Rome at the time of Caesar's assassination, which then involved Mark Antony escorting her out of Rome. She was no fool and understood that Octavian, Caesar's named heir, was a threat to her son Caesarion. She wisely chose to return to Egypt immediately.

Octavian Declares Victory

Octavian (Born 63BC - 14AD)
After the Battle of Actium circa 30BC

THE LOVE AFFAIR of Cleopatra and Mark Antony was necessary propaganda set in motion by Octavian. He needed to vilify Cleopatra, just as today politicians vilify heads of state like Saddam Hussein, Assad, Vladimir Putin in Russia or Xi Jinping in China. It is a strategy from ancient times—vilify your opponent to embolden the people to follow you into war. The vilification of Cleopatra and the character assassination wielded against Mark Antony was all necessary to justify war.

Octavian also had his mission to seize power. After stripping Lepidus of power by getting his armies to defect to him, he had turned to the pro-Antony Senate of Rome and flipped their loyalty as well. To accomplish that, he claimed to have obtained Antony's "supposed" will that disclosed his foreign-born children as heirs and displayed further disloyalty to Rome by requesting burial at Alexandria with Cleopatra. That was illegal, but it worked. Cleopatra had indeed met her match—Octavian.

Octavian (27 BC-14 AD)
EGYPT, Alexandria Æ 80 Drachmae (17.76 grams)
First series struck circa 30-27 BC. Bare head right; [Θ]EOV-YIOY
Rev: [KAICAPOC] AYTOKPATOPOC, eagle standing left
Cornucopiae before, Π behind. Dattari 2

ArmstrongEconomics.COM

After Cleopatra's death, Octavian began to issue Egyptian coinage replacing Cleopatra's portrait with his own. He began to issue these coins virtually immediately after her death in 30 BC. This was a declaration to all Egyptians and the world that Octavian conquered Egypt. Moreover, the final surrender of Egypt and the death of Cleopatra also mark, historically, the final demise of the Hellenistic Age as well as the Ptolemaic Kingdom.

Octavian took complete control of Alexandria and executed Mark Antony, Jr., his son by Fulvia, who was also in Alexandria with his father at the time. He did allow their daughter Cleopatra Selene to live, and he took her to Rome since she was only five years old at the time. As for Caesarion, son of Cleopatra and Julius Caesar born in 47 BC, he too was executed in 30 BC. Thus, Octavian emerged as the undisputed head of the Roman Empire at the age of thirty-three.

Mark Antony & Mark Antony, Jr.
AV Aureus

Octavian
(63-27BC)
AV Aureus struck 28BC
Crocodile right with AEGVPT above, CAPTA below
announce his victory over Egypt without mentioning Marc Antony
ArmstrongEconomics.COM

The Roman coinage issued by Octavian to celebrate his victory was carefully crafted to make no mention of his victory over Mark Antony. He was not celebrating victory over Mark Antony, a once-beloved Roman whom Octavian saw as a manipulated love fool. He was celebrating his defeat of Cleopatra and releasing propaganda to promote his success in battle. Thus, he issued his coinage displaying a crocodile, declaring Egypt was captive in both gold and silver.

Octavian - Egypt Captive
Octavian invaded Egypt in August 30 BC
ArmstrongEconomics.COM

Thus, Octavian's victory at the Battle of Actium resulted in him securing sole, uncontested control of Roman Empire. This victory enabled him to consolidate his power over every institution of Roman administration.

Then the question was how to seize complete control of Rome, yet not be assassinated as Julius Caesar for accepting the title of Dictator for Life.

Julius Caesar (100-44BC)
"DICT PERPETVO"
Perpetual Dictator
ArmstrongEconomics.COM

How to solve this dilemma was a critical political decision. When you buy insurance, it is always labeled with some disaster like fire,

RIC 407

theft, accident, and even health care to cover costs. But when it came to selling death insurance, people thought it might be bad luck. So, they changed the name to life insurance and people bought it.

The question was how to effectively become a king when Rome had revolted against a king to create the Republic in 509 BC. The office of dictator was traditionally for just one year. A new label for dictator had to be created to mask the same position of power. The Senate was convinced to create another title which was less offensive. Octavian was given the title Augustus on January 16, 27 BC, on his own insistence. It meant "first among citizens," or the venerable. This formally ended the Republic and ushered in Imperial Rome. He combined that with taking the name Caesar as well.

Augustus sought to buy approval of the people with his *Res Gestae*, which illustrated his skill of manipulation.

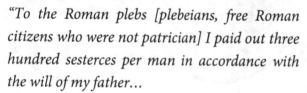

"To the Roman plebs [plebeians, free Roman citizens who were not patrician] I paid out three hundred sesterces per man in accordance with the will of my father...

To the municipal towns I paid money for the lands which I assigned to soldiers... paid for lands in the provinces was about two hundred and sixty million. I was the first and only one to do this...

I freed the sea from pirates... The whole of Italy voluntarily took oath of allegiance to me and demanded me as its leader in the war in which I was victorious at Actium."

Res Gestae Divi Augusti, 15,16 & 25

Juba II (25 BC-23 AD) was King of Mauretania and the son of King Juba I of Numidia. His father had supported Pompey against Caesar in Africa and continued to support the Pompeiians even after the death of Pompey. Following Caesar's victory, Juba I fled to Zama after the Battle of Thapsus, where he had a slave kill him. But his son, Juba II, was taken to Rome in 46 BC as a child, following the death of his father. There he lived under the protection of both Caesar and Octavian while he was educated in Roman tradition.

Juba II of Mauretania & Cleopatra VII
AR Denarius 3.02 grams SNG 566
ArmstrongEconomics.COM

Juba II was extremely intelligent and quickly gained the reputation of being one of the most learned men in the world. He became an early supporter of Octavian in his war against Marc Antony and Cleopatra. In 30 BC, following Octavian's conquest of Egypt, Juba II was married to Cleopatra Selene, the daughter of Marc Antony and the Egyptian Queen Cleopatra. Here again, is a coin depicting his mother-in-law.

Queen Cleopatra Selene (25BC-24AD)
Daughter of Cleopatra VII and Mark Antony also wife of Juba II
AR Denarius (3.45 grams) Caesarea mint
Diademed and draped bust left / Bull, head surmounted by globe

ArmstrongEconomics.COM

Juba's marriage to their daughter, Cleopatra Selene, was clearly political in nature. Octavian did not seek to kill Antony or his heirs for political appearance. We can see the resemblance in her portrait on this denarius from Mauretania. Octavian sought a means by which he could stabilize Africa.

Octavian allowing Juba II to depict Cleopatra and her daughter on coinage was an effort to imply that her bloodline was not extinguished. Octavian hoped that this would ease some of the tension in North Africa, feeling that the days of Alexander the Great were not extinguished.

For you see, even though Rome had conquered all of Greece, Asia, and North Africa, they retained their monetary system of Alexander the Great based on the drachma. During the days of Alexander the Great, the standard denomination was the Tetradrachm, struck in silver. This was the equivalent of four drachmae. Here is a cistophorus issued by Augustus at the Pergamum Mint in modern Turkey. It was the equivalent of three denarii. Even the monetary system clung to the days of the Greek empire.

Diocletian (284-305 AD) instituted a monetary reform throughout the Empire in 296 AD. This time, he also applied this to all of Asia including Egypt in 297/298 AD. Diocletian's reform ended the Egyptian closed currency system, under which it had functioned for the previous 600 years. It was introduced by Alexander the Great when he conquered Egypt in 332-330 BC and unified the Empire monetarily under one set of coinages. Therefore, this terminated the run of Egyptian tetradrachms which had long been reduced with inflation from silver to bronze.

Octavian understood the underlying tension throughout the former Greek Empire and that the death of Cleopatra was the end of an era. There were concerns that the East could rise because of this event. For this reason, Octavian sent the prince Juba II to rule his own people. In 25 AD, Octavian, now known as Augustus (27 BC-14 AD), traded Juba II for Numidia, which had long been a source of gold for the Egyptians.

Augustus (27BC - 14AD)
AR Cistophorus (Capricorn)
Pergamum Mint RIC 493 (11.89 grams)
Cistophorus = 3 Drachms = 3 Denarii
ArmstrongEconomics.COM

The Numidians were among the ancestors of modern Berbers. By the time of their incorporation into the Roman military, they had been living side-by-side with the Carthaginians, who were of Phoenician origin, for several centuries. There was a lot of intermixing in both directions. Nevertheless, they did not share this historical tie to the good old days of Alexander the Great. The ancient sources don't really give 'color' information of the various people. All we do know is that they typically distinguished Libya—basically, Africa west of Egypt and north of the Sahara from Aethiopia—which was inhabited peoples they thought of as darker-skinned.

Diocletian (284-305AD)
Æ Tetradrachm (Egypt)
Monetary Reform od 297/298AD ended
600 years of Greek Monetary System in Egypt
ArmstrongEconomics.COM

Consequently, swapping Juba Numidia for Mauretania was intended to create the impression that the bloodline of Alexander the Great continued. Juba II was an intellectual, as was his new queen, Cleopatra Selene. Juba's reliance upon Rome to ensure that he would retain the throne in the face of public unrest was critical. Even to issue coins with Cleopatra Selene's portrait demonstrated she had his utmost respect.

King Ptolemy of Mauretania (circa 20-40AD)
AR Denarius (1.68 grams) Caesarea mint
Dated RY 6 (circa 25/6 or 26/7AD)
Diademed and draped bust of Ptolemy right
Rev: Draped curule chair, surmounted by laurel wreath

Grandon of Antony & Cleopatra

ArmstrongEconomics.COM

As previously mentioned, Ptolemy of Mauretania was therefore the grandson of Mark Antony and Cleopatra. He reigned until 40 AD, when Emperor Caligula (37-41 AD) invited him to Rome and had him executed. In truth, the bloodline to Mark Antony meant that there was a blood connection to Ptolemy. Thanks to Caligula, the final bloodline that had any connection to Cleopatra and her Macedonian roots was extinguished.

Augustus
(27BC -14AD)
AR Denarius (20mm, 3.55 grams)

A comet that appeared in summer 44 BC was held to signal Julius Caesar's ascension to the heavens and proved quite useful in Octavian's effort to get the Senate to deify his adoptive father. The memory of Caesar's deification was revived in connection with Augustus' proposal to hold the Saecular Games in 17 BC and the "Julian star" is featured on coinage in the years leading up to the event.

Octavian began to issue coins with the name Augustus. He also issued coins stating that Julius Caesar was divine. The coinage featured a design of a comet that had appeared when he was assassinated, which became known as the "Julian Star." The appearance of a comet was seen as a mark of a great ruler. That was also applied to the Star of Bethlehem and the birth of Christ.

Furthermore, to commemorate his victory over Antony, Augustus established the Roman festival Actia. Augustus set up a Victory Monument overlooking the site, which incorporated the bronze rams taken from the defeated ships. The surviving sockets in the stonework are physical evidence of the size of these rams.

Augustus (27BC - 14Ad)
AV Aureus Victory holding Shield
ArmstrongEconomics.COM

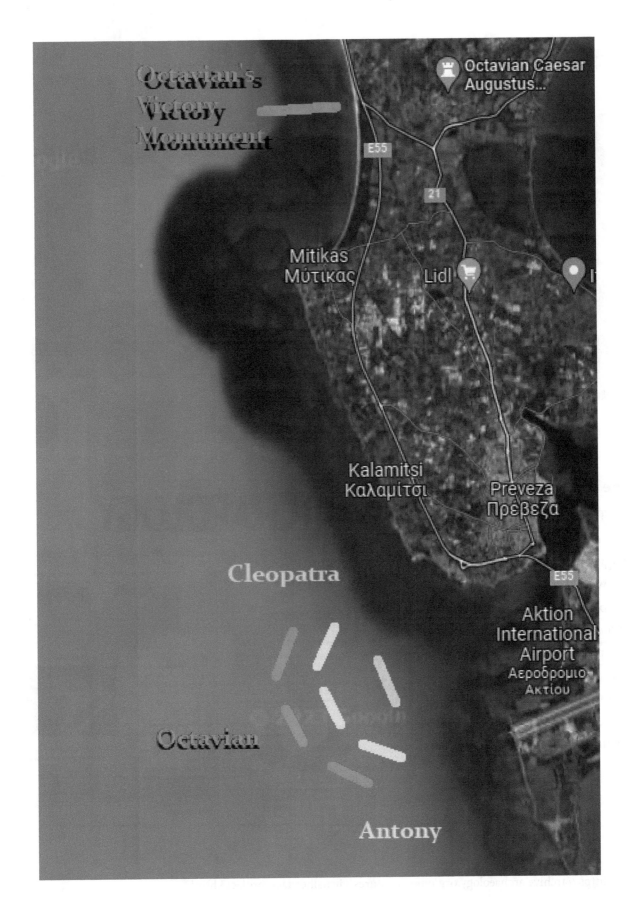

The Victory Monument of Actium

The Victory Monument of Actium was constructed on the campsite where Augustus was prior to the battle. We know that this was constructed thanks to brief passages from both Cassius Dio and Suetonius. The architectural composition of the monument implies that Augustus claimed his victory was divine intervention in the naval battle's outcome. *Archaeology*[4] has published a virtual model of what it looked like.

ARCHAEOLOGY   Archive

A publication of the Archaeological Institute of America

HOME   NEWS   MAGAZINE   VIDEOS   PODCASTS   READER INFO   TRAVEL   SUBSCRIBE

online features

Why do Virtual Heritage?

by Donald H. Sanders

March 13, 2008

The Monument at Actium

In 31 B.C., Mark Antony and Cleopatra fought Octavian (later Augustus) in the crucial naval battle during their war for control of the Roman world. The two fleets clashed along the western coast of Greece, just outside the Ambracian Gulf. A nearby cape, Actium, gave the battle its name, and two years after the victory, Augustus built a monument in thanksgiving on the heights overlooking the waters where the battle had been waged. The monument has a stone wall into one side of which were set bronze rams cut off the bows of Antony and Cleopatra's ships.

Screen grabs from the virtual reality model of the Athlit ram, showing the ram shape and the rear outline of the

The oddly shaped cuttings in the Actium monument's wall are large and deep and seem to represent the negative shape of the backs of the rams. Each "socket" is unique in its size and shape, reflecting the dimensions of the actual rams at the point of contact with the wall. One goal of the project was to develop a virtual reality model that would give visitors to the planned site museum an appreciation for the massiveness of the bronze rams and an understanding of the general design of the monument.

Rendering of the monument at Actium showing a reconstruction of the main features, including the row of bronze rams protruding from the main wall of the complex (© 2003 Institute for the Visualization of History, Inc.)

---

4   https://archive.archaeology.org/online/features/virtualheritage/project3.html

Augustus & Agrippa Æ As of Nemausus, Gaul
struck 10-14AD Head of Agrippa to left, Augustus right
Chained crocodile & palm COL NEM across fields RIC 159
Refers directly to the victory at Actium over Cleopatra VII & Mark Antony
ArmstrongEconomics.COM

Over the years, we continue to find coinage commemorating the victory at Actium and the defeat of Cleopatra. Here is an artistically fascinating and unique coin which refers directly to the victory of Octavian and Agrippa at Actium over the forces of Cleopatra VII and Marc Antony. Veterans were given land in Nemausus, Gaul (modern-day Nimes, France).

The crocodile, collared around the neck and chained to a palm on the reverse of this coin, is a clear reference to the subjugation of Egypt, thus obliquely referring also to Antony and Cleopatra. The wreath above with ties fluttering in the breeze is a reminder that the war was both just and necessary, with the victory having brought about the deliverance and salvation of the Roman people and the empire.

It is noteworthy also that the portraits of Agrippa and Augustus on the obverse are presented on the same level and back-to-back, at once recalling the ancient Janiform types once so prevalent on the Roman coinage, and presenting princeps and general as inseparable and heroic partners—one adorned with a wreath of laurel, the other with a rostral wreath in recognition for his naval victories.

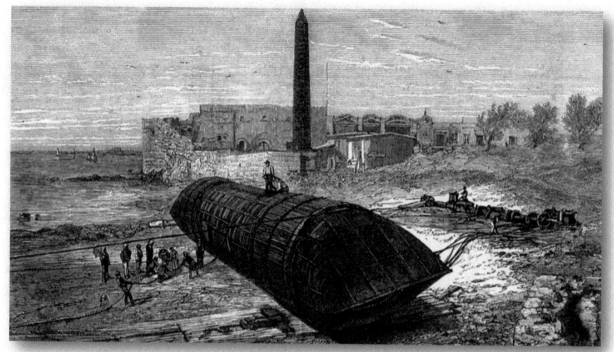

Transporting Cleopatra's Needles from the Caesareum - 1877
Illustrated London News Ltd

As for Cleopatra's Caesareum dedicated to Julius Caesar to legitimatize her claim to Rome, it was completed and expanded by Augustus, after he defeated Mark Antony and Cleopatra in Egypt. There were two obelisks that have been known as Cleopatra's Needles. They were given as gifts to London and New York. Cleopatra never saw them. They were set up more than 3,000 years ago in Heliopolis. An old record survived which confirms that they were moved to Alexandria by Augustus about 15 BC, fifteen to sixteen years after her death.

Augustus rededicated the Caesareum to his family. The busts were all carved in the rare Egyptian black basalt stone. Only a few have survived, which certainly would not have been carried out on the orders of Cleopatra. She dedicated this to Julius Caesar only for political purposes.

Here is a bust of Germanicus who was born twenty-nine years

Germanicus Julius Caesar
(15BC - 19AD)

after Caesar's death and fifteen years after the death of Cleopatra. This is further evidence that Augustus rededicated the temple.

Just as the damage was done to the bust of Caesar, we find the same attempt to deface this bust of Germanicus as well. They also carved a cross in his forehead. The Christians were ignorant. They went about destroying sculptures and defacing them under the false idea that they were pagan gods. There is also a black basalt bust of Livia, Augustus's wife, in the Louvre. These busts appear to have been taken to southern France during Napoleon's invasion of Egypt.

Without question, this black basalt portrait of Julius Caesar was obviously the first established on the orders of Cleopatra herself, to support her political ambitions. There are only about twenty genuine surviving portraits of Caesar. All the other busts that were in this Caesareum were added by Augustus after his victory. Some elements of the temple survived until the nineteenth century. Cleopatra's Needles, the two obelisks, were taken from this temple in 1877. They now stand in Central Park in New York City, and on the Thames Embankment in London. The obelisk at the Vatican was taken from the Karnak Temple and once stood in the Circus Maximus.

Napoleon in Egypt (1798–1801)

Nevertheless, it does seem that the surviving black basalt busts of Caesar, Germanicus, and Livia were part of the same imperial portrait group. The iconographical considerations, the distinctive and rare Egyptian material, the size, and similarity of workmanship suggest that they were all undoubtedly produced by the same workshop. The nature and degree of damage by Christians is also consistent. Additionally, their reported association with the same collection in Southern France suggests that they were brought back to France during the Napoleonic campaign.

Professor of Classical Art and Archaeology John Pollini of the University of Southern California confirms that the bust of Caesar was the one established in Alexandria. It stood with "other members of the Julio-Claudian family [that] were once set up in a shrine, [and] they would have been even more likely targets of Christian fanaticism. In any case, the aggregate of evidence argues for our 'magnificent basalt head' being a portrait of Julius Caesar that was freely interpreted by some Hellenistic sculptor working in Alexandria at the very end of the Republic or in the earlier Augustan period."

One of the most famous philosophers of all time, as well as a mathematician, was a woman named Hypatia (c. 350/370-415 AD) who was murdered at the Caesareum by a Christian mob in 415 AD. She was a prominent and brilliant thinker of her day in Alexandria. She taught philosophy and astronomy but the Christians who feared science out of their ignorance persecuted her.

MORT DE LA PHILOSOPHE HYPATIE, A ALEXANDRIE

According to Socrates Scholasticus, a mob of Christians dragged Hypatia from her carriage into the Caesareum, a pagan temple converted into a Christian church by that time as they also did with the Pantheon in Rome. She was stripped and murdered by stoning. The Caesareum had been the headquarters of Cyril of Alexandria, the Patriarch of Alexandria from 412 to 444 AD at the time of her murder.

As I have said, these legionary denarii of Mark Antony was one of the largest productions of Roman coins to the extent that they remained in circulation and have been discovered in hoards even up to 250 years later, although highly worn. This is why we will also find examples nearly worn smooth.

Once again, this was a confirmation of just how extensive this issue was to fund Cleopatra's bold attempt to conquer Rome and reestablish the Kingdom of Alexander the Great.

Mark Antony's Legions

LEG V - Crawford 544/30

THE MOST ENDURING aspect of this epic Battle of Actium is the remarkable coinage of Mark Antony funded by Cleopatra VII. What appears to have been a strategic maneuver for propaganda purposes, Mark Antony struck coinage primarily in silver for each legion, but also a few gold aurei have survived for the commanders of each legion. The most common will be that of Legion VI and the rarest are IIX, XIV, XIIX, XVIII, and those XXIV and higher.

The Roman legion was the largest military unit within the Roman army. It was composed of 5,200 infantry and 300 equites (cavalry) during this period. After the Battle of Actium, the basic legion was increased to 5,600 infantry and 200 auxilia post-27 BC when Octavian became Augustus.

Marcus Antonius - Legion XX Aureus

The "legionary denarii" of Marcus Antonius are one of the most interesting historical pieces of evidence from this period. They are certainly among the most recognizable and collectible of all ancient coins of this period that reaffirm history. Many have survived, and they appear to have been in circulation at least 100 years later. They are often found to be very worn as a result.

MARCUS AURELIUS. AR "Legionary" Denarius Restitution
Commemorative issued 168 AD commemorating the 200th anniversary
of the battle of Actium (3.60 gm)

ArmstrongEconomics.COM

Marcus Aurelius (161-180 AD) issued a commemorative in 168 AD, showing just how significant they remained even 200 years later. They may have remained in circulation for a long time because the silver coinage began to be debased with the Great Fire of Rome in 64 AD under Emperor Nero (54-68 AD) to pay for the crisis. It is possible that these legionary denarii may have carried a special premium following Nero for Emperor Trajan (97-117 AD), who recalled all old silver coinage and melted them down, issuing new coinage that was debased to pay for the Dacian War in 107 AD.

Here is a worn example counterstamped during the civil war that followed the death of Nero in 68 AD. It is counterstamped "IMP VES" of Emperor Vespasian (69-79 AD). Once again, this shows that they remained in circulation for 100 years that can be verified.

Mark Antony Legion III
Counterstamp "IMP VES" applied at Ephesus (74-79AD)
Howgego 839

ArmstrongEconomics.COM

These legionary denarii are indeed of great historical importance in addition to being an iconic legend that is familiar even to those who are not ancient coin collectors. The Battle of Actium and love affair of Antony and Cleopatra has been an enduring story for centuries.

It was Cleopatra who convinced Antony to confront Octavian on the sea, for she possessed a large fleet. Antony was more of a strategic ground fighter, not a navy man. That was his downfall. Cleopatra funded the war exploiting a division between Antony and Octavian.

The entire purpose of this coinage that was struck with the wealth of Egypt was to intimidate Octavian by striking coinage for each legion which may, or may not, have existed. This was obviously a strategy of propaganda for all of Rome, suggesting that his army was vast, and he held support of most Roman people.

The coinage that is found in quantity covers Legions I to XXIII. These are the coins that are also often found worn, showing that they remained in circulation for many years. This suggests that Antony's legions had amounted to just under 200,000 men if we rely on the coinage. This appears to have been a brilliant move for propaganda.

Quite remarkable—here is an obverse die, made of bronze within an iron sheath for a legionary denarius. It is the only known die to have survived.

MARK ANTONY Legionary Die Circa 32 BC
Obverse die, bronze within iron sheath, for a Legionary Denarius
Dimensions: length, 26mm; width, 24mm, weight: 57.61 grams
Incuse - ANT. AVG. III VIR. R. P. C, galley to the right

Marcus Antonius
AR Denarius (bare hd rt/"ANTONIVS AVG IMP III")
Crawford 542/2

ArmstrongEconomics.COM

Mark Antony produced a wide variety of coin types following the assassination of Caesar in 44 BC until his own demise in 31 BC. We certainly find much rarer issues that have survived displaying his portrait with that of Julius Caesar. This was clearly an issue to gain support that he was Caesar's right hand, not this boy upstart by the name of Octavian.

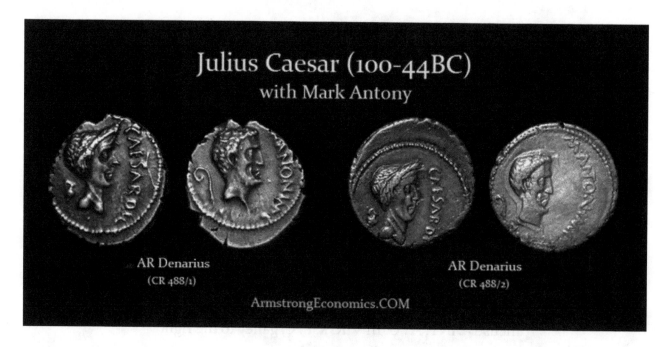

Julius Caesar (100-44BC)
with Mark Antony

AR Denarius
(CR 488/1)

AR Denarius
(CR 488/2)

ArmstrongEconomics.COM

There is also an extremely rare issue of gold aurei that have survived of Antony with his son Mark Antony, Jr. with his third wife Fulvia. It was Fulvia's daughter from her prior marriage who married Octavian (the future Augustus).

Mark Antony & Lucius Antonius
AV Aureus
ArmstrongEconomics.COM

Fulvia, in her own right, was politically active. She conspired with Lucius Antonius to rebel against Octavian. Perhaps she did this to get her husband to return to Italy and abandon Cleopatra.

Nevertheless, the legionary type without question is the coinage that has indeed survived the ravages of time and circumstance rendering them perhaps the most common coinage to have survived from Mark Antony and Cleopatra. The bulk of the legionary denarii from his many twenty-three regular legions with two specialized units were the ancient version of the CIA (the praetorian cohorts and the cohort of speculatores). In addition, three legions were honored with supplementary issues that also refer to their title: XII Antiqvae, XVII Classicae, and XVIII Lybicae.

Gold legionary aurei appear to have been a very limited issue. Surviving examples are rare. This tends to imply that Antony's ability to pay in gold was strained, or it was limited to the officers. Surely, Cleopatra could have provided a substantial amount of gold. The scarcity of gold legionary aurei suggests that it was confined to the commanders of the legions.

Mark Antony
Legionary Aureus
CHORTIVM PRAETORIARVM

When we look at the silver content of Antony's legionary denarii, we find that their silver fineness was 92%, following the Asian standard, which was much lower than contemporary denarii struck at Rome that were about 97% fine at that point in time. This may explain why they remained in circulation for so long. They may have often been discounted by bankers accepting them but paying them out at full value. That may have changed with Nero's debasement in 64 AD, which was from 97.5% to about 93.5%.

Mark Antony - Legionary Aureus - Legion XIII

The gold legionary aurei appear to have been confined to the commanders of eight legions that we can confirm. They were simply not issued in any quantity. Michael Crawford, in his spectacular book *Roman Republican Coinage*, records Legions IV, VI, XII, XIII, XIV, and XIX in addition to the Praetorians. There have been some that Crawford failed to note in his 1974 publication such as the 1955 find of Legion II. In addition, Legion XX has also appeared.

A Legionary denarius of Mark Antony Legion III
Countermarked "MP VES" by Vespasian during his 4th counsulship (72-73AD)
Struck at Ephesus and circulated specifically within the province of Asia Minor.
Implies the denarii were countermarked to validate locally circulating silver coinage

ArmstrongEconomics.COM

Marc Antony struck his silver 'legionary' coinage in very large quantities as he and Queen Cleopatra VII prepared for war with Octavian and Agrippa. To fund his army, as many as thirty-nine emissions were produced. As stated, the total amount of coinage was most likely more than 25 million denarii.

Remarkably, when Vesuvius erupted, burying Pompeii and surrounding cities in 79 AD, Antony's legionary denarii accounted for 20% of the coins found in Pompeii more than 100 years later. This tends to confirm that the sheer magnitude of the issue was staggering. This Battle at Actium on a monetary level was certainly the ancient equivalent of World War II. The drastic amount of coinage produced was on a monumental scale for these coins to have still been 20% of the money supply just over 100 years later.

Further evidence that these denarii were in circulation at the time of the destruction of Pompeii is this worn denarius countermarked during the civil war period, as previously mentioned. Here we have an Antony legionary denarius, Legion III, countermarked "MP VES" by Vespasian (69-79 AD), which is dated to the emperor's fourth consulship (72-73 AD). The countermark suggests a starting date of 74 AD for this countermark's use in Asia. This countermark appears mostly on late Republican and Imperatorial denarii up to the time of Nero.

1905 Delos Hoard	
CHOR SPECVL	9
CHOR PRAET.....	6
XII ANTIQVAE	5
XVII CLASSICAE	8
XVIII LYBICAE	4
PRI	0
LEG II	40
LEG III	25
LEG IIII	0
LEG IV	28
LEG V	37
LEG VI	36
LEG VII	27
LEG VIII.............	27
LEG IIX	0
LEG VIIII.............	15
LEG IX	20
LEG X	28
LEG XI	24
LEG XII	28
LEG XIII	20
LEG XIIII	6
LEG XIV	12
LEG XV	39
LEG XVI	24
LEG XVII	22
LEG XVIII	6
LEG XVIIII	0
LEG XIX	16
LEG XX	13
LEG XXI	23
LEG XXII	15
LEG XXIII	24
Legion obscured ...	17
Total	604

The "**MP VES**" countermarks circulated specifically within the province of Asia Minor. There was little silver to mint coins in Asia at the time, so we see old denarii countermarked.

These countermarked denarii clearly had a purpose to validate their continued use of the coins locally as an acceptable weight. While the regional mints opened by Vespasian were gearing up production, we find that countermarking the cistophori, equal to three denarii, with the contemporary "**MP VES AVG**" and "**IMP VP NC**" seems to support this theory since they were not particularly as worn down as the legionary denarii. This was a validation.

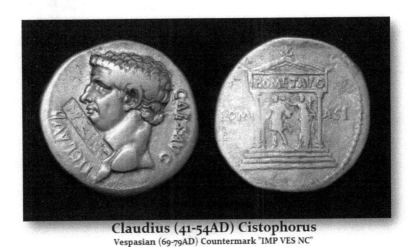

Claudius (41-54AD) Cistophorus
Vespasian (69-79AD) Countermark "IMP VES NC"
ArmstrongEconomics.COM

No other coin ever struck by the Romans formed such a long-lasting importance within the Roman Empire. What this all demonstrates is that the vast quantity of coins issued by Antony and Cleopatra exceeded a total mintage of at least 25 million and as much as 30 to 35 million coins. As mentioned, regarding the coins discovered at Pompeii, Antony's legionary denarii possibly made up 20% of all of the total denarii circulating in the Roman Empire during the reign of the Flavian emperors, Vespasian (69–79 AD), Titus (79-81 AD), and Domitian (81-96 AD).

There were hoards discovered around the site of the Battle of Actium. One such hoard was discovered in 1905 and is known as the Delos Hoard. It was unearthed during the excavations of the French School in a house near the theater on Delos. It consisted of 650 coins. There was a small group of Republican denarii from about 147 BC, forty in all. However, what dates the hoard is that there were 604 coins of Antony's legionary denarii.

The Delos Hoard shows that this was an individual who stashed his money during a time of war and did not survive to collect his coins. This was probably a soldier in Antony's legions. The importance of this is to demonstrate that one individual had coins from most of the legions. Perhaps he was engaging in money-dealing or gambling on the side. The two most common coins from this hoard were Legion II and Legion XV. The absent legions are the first, PRI, and Legions IIII, IIX, and XVIIII.

There were six legionary denarii in the 1934 Swaby Hoard discovered in England about eight miles south of Lincolnshire. The hoard is dated with the latest coin which was that of L. Aelius Caesar (136-138 AD), but the dominant coinage was that of Trajan (98-117 AD) followed by Hadrian (117-138 AD). It was Hadrian who ordered the wall to be constructed between England and Scotland.

C. Valerius Flaccus (82BC)
AR Denarius Draped and winged bust of Victory to right
Legionary eagle between two standards
Issued when he was Proconsul preparing Civil War Dictator Sulla

ArmstrongEconomics.COM

In contrast, the 2010 Nowa Wieś Głubczycka Hoard discovered in Upper Silesia in southern Poland contained Roman Republican coinage but no Antony legionary denarii. The latest coin discovered was countermarked by Vespasian. Yet, within the Roman Empire, there are additional later hoards, suggesting that even by the reign of Severus Alexander (222-235 AD), denarii of Antony's legions were still in circulation, albeit very worn.

In truth, Antony's legionary denarii were themselves inspired by the civil war involving the rise of the Dictator Sulla. The legionary design first appeared on the Republican coinage of C. Valerius Flaccus (82 BC) who was Sulla's proconsul in Gaul. His coinage was struck in Massilia to finance the ongoing revolt of Sertorius in Spain (80-72 BC). The legionary eagle and standards that appear here on the reverse is the first instance that it appeared on coins as the main

Cn. Nerius, L. Lentulus, Claudius Marcellus
AR Denarius 49BC (3.68 grams) Pay for Pompey's Troops Against Caesar
NERI·Q·VRB Head of Saturn right
L·LENT – [C·MARC] Legionary eagle between standard below, CO – S

design element. Subsequently, of course, it appears to have been used during civil wars to promote that the issuer had the support of the legions.

After Caesar crossed the Rubicon on January 10, 49 BC, we find this legionary design, implying civil war. This was issued in 49 BC by Cn. Nerius, L. Lentulus and Claudius Marcellus. Here, the obverse displayed the head of Saturn with the legionary design on the reverse. This design implied civil war. Crossing the Rubicon removed any doubt that the matter would have to be resolved by force of arms.

This denarius was issued to raise troops to face Caesar's far more experienced and dedicated army of veterans. To raise troops, they would need money, and this coin was part of an ad hoc issue intended for that purpose. These coins were issued by Gnaeus Nerius, a Quaestor Urbanus, who had charge of the Aerarium—the official treasury of the Roman Republic. That was the place where the military standards were kept, based in the Temple of Saturn in Rome. By naming the consuls of that year, they imply that Caesar is a usurper, and they were elected consuls. It was the last coin issued before Pompey and the corrupt senators fled for Asia and Caesar seized the mint.

The Triumvirs. Octavian. (Autumn 42 BC)
AR Denarius (3.80 grams) Military mint in Greece
Helmeted bust of Mars right/Aquila between two standards
Crawford 497/3

Antony introduced his legionary coinage, in addition to the legionary standards struck in about 82 BC by moneyer C. Valerius Flaccus. Then we find coinage of when Caesar crossed the Rubicon in 49 BC by Cn. Nerius. Upon the assassination of Caesar in 44 BC, we find that by 42 BC, Octavian issued a denarius with the head of Mars, the god of war, with the reverse displaying the legionary standards with the noted "S C" meaning with the sanction of the Senate. This was once again confirming a civil war and this time it was against the assassins of Caesar.

All the legionary denarii appear to have been struck between 32 and 31 BC while Antony

Marck Antony & Cleopatra VII
(83-30BC)   (69-30BC)
AR Silver Tetradrachm (11.12 grams)
ArmstrongEconomics.COM

was in Greece preparing for his war against Octavian. The silver content was that of Asia and was below Roman standards for the time. You can see the debasement of this Asian tetradram. The fact that they accounted for about 20% of the money supply up to 100 years later stands as evidence of the cost of that war to take control of the Roman Empire as Antony was a pawn of Cleopatra.

Here we have a rare denarius of Nero (54-68 AD) with reverse showing the standards. This again appears to stand for a symbol of civil war. Indeed, that is what took place in 68 AD.

NERO (54-68AD)
Rome, circa 67-68AD. IMP NERO CAESAR AVG P P
Laureate head of Nero to right (3.49 grams)
Rev. Legionary eagle with wings spread between two standards

ArmstrongEconomics.COM

Gaius Julius Vindex (c. 25–68 AD) was a Roman governor in the province of Gallia Lugdunensis (Central France). He was a member of the former royal family of Aquitania, which lost its throne during the conquest of Gaul by Julius Caesar. Nonetheless, his family remained highly influential in the region. His father became a Roman senator after Emperor Claudius (41-54 AD) had permitted noblemen from Gaul to enter the Senate.

Vindex was shocked by Nero's behavior. In late 58 AD, Nero's mother, Agrippina Jr., (15-59 AD) and a group of soldiers and senators were accused of attempting to overthrow Nero. It was said that they planned to move with Gaius Rubellius Plautus (33–62 AD), who was related to the Julio-Claudian family, and the grandson of Drusus, the only son of Tiberius. Since his great-grandmothers were Vipsania Agrippina and Antonia Minor, he was also descended from Marcus Agrippa and Mark Antony.

Nero & Mother Agrippina, Jr.
AV Gold Aureus - Facing Busts
ArmstrongEconomics.COM

Vindex appears to be one of the men plotting with Nero's mother to overthrow him and initially place Plautus on the throne. The circumstances of Agrippina's death in 59 AD on March 23 remains uncertain. The bias against Nero generated so much fake news, we really do not know what happened.

In either late 67 or early 68 AD, Vindex finally rebelled against Emperor Nero. Unlike other usurpers, Vindex, as a senator, only sought to

Gaius Julius Vindex
(c. 25–68AD)
ArmstrongEconomics.COM

replace Nero with a better candidate. The coinage that he issued NEVER displayed his portrait. It was always promoting the Empire. Here, too, we find this same reverse with the standard which was the same theme as Mark Antony without noting a legion. This design appears during civil wars—not mere international war, or even a usurpation.

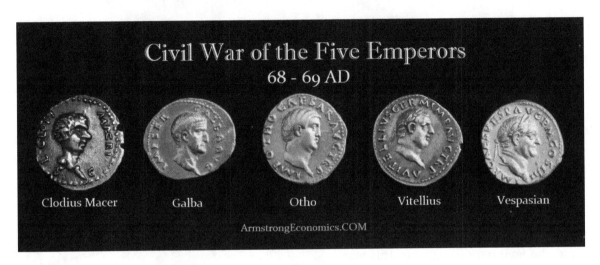

Vindex revolted against Nero and encouraged Galba (68-69 AD), governor of Hispania, to claim the Empire. Vindex was defeated by the Rhine legions. Nero committed suicide on June 9, 68 AD, after the Senate declared him a public enemy, raising Galba to the throne. Otho (69 AD) had supported Galba but when Galba passed over him as an heir, he killed him on January 15, 69 AD and seized the throne for himself. In Africa, Clodius Macer (68 AD) also rebelled.

Vitellius (69 AD) was hailed by the Rhine legions on January 1, 69 AD and defeated Otho, who then committed suicide. The Senate then proclaimed Vitellius as the Emperor on April 19 when Vespasian (69-79 AD), then in Syria, was proclaimed by the legions and was hailed Emperor in Alexandria, Egypt, on July 1. Rather than fight, his troops killed Vitellius, leaving Vespasian as the emperor.

We find this design also appeared on the coinage of Clodius Macer (68 AD) during the civil war, as Antony did, noting LEG III that followed the death of Nero in 68 AD. We find that it reappears on various other issues.

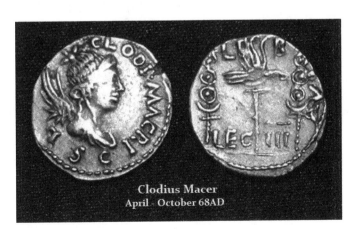

Clodius Macer
April - October 68AD

We find that the Flavian emperors also displayed the legionary design but this was regarding the conquest of Judaea, which was also a civil war. The Judaea had erupted in a civil war of their own with factions divided against one another. Sicarii, led by Menahem ben Judah, could hold on while the Zealots, initially led by Eleazar ben Simon, were unstable. Of course, the Arch of Titus at the head of the Roman Forum shows the looting of the Temple.

Titus besieged Jerusalem and surrounded the city. Yet Jewish raids by the Zealots nearly resulted in Titus being captured. This design

Titus (79-81AD)
AR Cistophoric Tetradrachm (10.70 grams) RIC 74
Legionary standards adopted
Jews had become embroiled in a civil war of their own
ArmstrongEconomics.COM

had suggested there was a civil war involved. Appearing on the Cistophori suggested it was in Asia not Rome.

The legionary design remained popular as it became a standard, appearing on the reverse of Imperial cistophori in Asia Minor. Here is a cistophori of Trajan (97-117 AD), still using this legionary design. Trajan also used it for coins in all metals. Quadrantes with this type were struck anonymously.

Trajan (97-117AD)
AR Cistophorus (10.96 grams) RIC719
ArmstrongEconomics.COM

Caracalla (198-217AD)
Fides Militum standing to left between two standards

Trajan
(98 - 117AD)
SPQR OPTIMO PRINCIPI
Aquila between vexillum and standard
ArmstrongEconomics.COM

Elagabalus (218-222)
AR Denarius Laureate bust right
Rev: FIDES MILITVM
Aquila (legionary eagle) flanked by two standar

Hadrian 118AD
Commemorating 150th anniversary of Actium
Æ As Laureate bust to right/aquila between two standards

Trajan issued a similar design in the denarii, but it is a modification of the Antony version and did not refer to a civil war. This was a striking departure in the use of this basic design.

Hadrian (117-138 AD) issued this bronze as in 118 AD to commemorate the 150th anniversary of the Battle of Actium. That is certainly what marked the birth of Imperial Rome and the end of the Republic.

This was followed by a restitution issue of Marcus Aurelius (161-180 AD) which was the 200th anniversary issue of the Battle of Actium. So, the original Antony issue of legionary denarii have been found in hoards even up to 250 years later. Once again, this was a confirmation of just how this issue was regarded by the people as well as its significant production.

As we continue to look at the issue of coinage from this point onward in time, we see that this

Marcus Aurelius & Lucius Verus
(161-180AD)
Commemorative Legionary Denarius Legion VI
ArmstrongEconomics.COM

design also reappears under Septimius Severus (193-211 AD) during the next civil war.

It is obvious that this is not just an issue to boost morale of the troops, but clearly propaganda to the rest of the empire that he has the support of the legions. What emerges here is that in both cases, the valid emperor was dead—Nero, in the first instance, and Commodus in the second. Therefore, these were coins issued not as a usurper, but a contender against other viable candidates in a void. They are clearly displaying a propaganda message that they have the support of the legions.

Septimius Severus
(193-211AD)
ArmstrongEconomics.COM

Some have attributed Caracalla (198-217 AD) as modifying the design with *Fides Militum,* who was the goddess of loyalty of the military, standing between two standards (signum). This symbolism did not have the same meaning. We find the same theme on this denarius of Elagabalus (219-222 AD). This is celebrating the military as the backbone of the strength of the Roman Empire.

The next time we find a series of coinage noting the distinct legions within the Roman military arrives during the reign of Gallienus (253-268 AD). It was his father who was captured by the Persians in 260 AD.

A bas relief at Naghsh-e Rostam, Shiraz, Iran with Shapur I on horseback showing Roman Emperor Valerian held captive chained to the wall who he eventually had stuffed as a trophy

This series for each legion notes their mascot and was intended to boost their morale rather than display support of the legions during a civil war. It was also to seek the protection of the gods in the face of the major crisis with the first emperor to be captured by the enemy. There is obviously a major distinction of the legionary denarii of Gallienus, compared to Antony, Macer, and Severus.

Gallienus' Legions

Gallienus. AD 253-268. Antoninianus
(21mm, 3.17 g, 12h). Mediolanum (Milan) mint. Issue 2(2)
AD 260-1 LEG IIII FL VI P VI F, lion leaping right

Gallienus. AD 253-268. Antoninianus
(23mm, 4.62 g, 6h). Mediolanum (Milan) mint. Issue 2(2)
AD 260-1 LEG VII CL VI P VI F, bull standing right.

Gallienus. AD 253-268. Antoninianus
(19.5mm, 3.01 g, 5h). Mediolanum (Milan) mint. Issue 2(2)
AD 260-1. LEG XIIII GEM

ArmstrongEconomics.COM

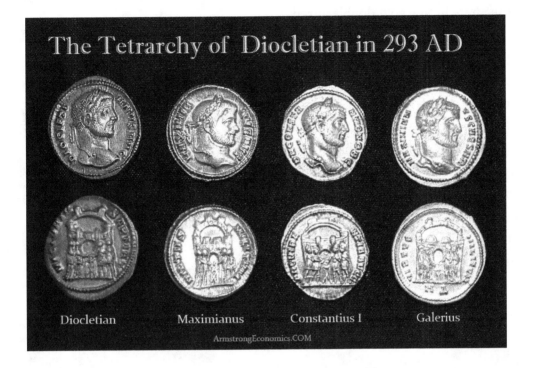

The Tetrarchy of Diocletian in 293 AD

Diocletian   Maximianus   Constantius I   Galerius

ArmstrongEconomics.COM

Following Gallienus, we arrive at the major reform of the Tetrarchy. These four emperors are pictured here as the cornerstone of Saint Mark's Cathedral in Venice. The empire was divided into four districts, each ruled separately. The goal was to end civil wars and establish a clear path of succession. Emperor Diocletian and Maximianus retired in 305 AD, the first emperors ever to do that. While this form of government was meant to endure, Constantine waged a series of civil wars, eventually ending the reform. He emerged as the sole ruler, claiming that there was one God; therefore, there should be one emperor. He used Christianity as a political path to power.

After Constantius I died, his son Constantine I the Great (307-337 AD), one member of this Tetrarchy, did not want to share any power. There was a major civil war when Constantine sought to defeat the other members of the Tetrarchy, which had been a major reform established by Diocletian (284-305 AD). The Tetrarchy was established in 293 AD, consisting of four different rulers, two head emperors (originally Diocletian and Maximianus) (284-305 AD) and two junior emperors who would be the heirs of Constantius I, the father of Constantine I, and Galerius.

Tetrarchy (293-305AD)
Diocletian & Maximianus as Emperors
Galerius & Constantius as Caesars
(located in Venice)

We can see here in this gold double aureus that he modified the design of Mark Antony and displayed himself standing between the two standards. This only celebrated his thirst for raw power. As for his claim that he saw a sign of the cross in the sky and had his army paint that on their shields, he knew that he was outnumbered and that Maxentius had built the first Christian church in Rome. Adopting the cross undermined Maxentius, whose army were mostly Christians who could not kill a fellow Christian.

AU Double Aureus

Constantine I the Great (307-337AD)
as Caesar 306-307AD
ArmstrongEconomics.COM

Constantine the Great's Vision of the Cross by Raphel

Constantine pretended he saw this vision of a cross in the sky because he knew most soldiers in the opposing force were Christian. He used Christianity to justify war by declaring there was one God so there should be only one emperor.

He further used Christianity as the excuse to confiscate all the wealth from the pagan temples to fund building Constantinople. On top of that, for someone who had such a vision, he waited to be baptized on his deathbed. He previously had no problem issuing coins with him in the image of a pagan god, such as Sol Invictus.

Maximinus II Daza
(305-308AD)

As Caesar AV Aureus (5.2 grams)
Maximinus standing left, holding globe two legionary standards behind

ArmstrongEconomics.COM

Maximinus II Daza (305-308 AD) was born to the sister of Emperor Galerius, making him his uncle. Here is an aureus showing himself with the standards behind him as he holds the world in his right hand. He was a committed pagan and engaged in Christian persecutions. He died of disease. Christian historians were not reliable; they ascribed death to everything from poison to divine justice.

Licinius I (308-324 AD) issued a coin with the design of Mark Antony, but with the legend on the reverse that identifies him as *Optimo Principi*, the best of emperors.

Licinius I
(308-324AD)

S P Q R OPTIMO PRINCIPI, Legionary eagle left between two standards
Optimo Principi = the best of emperors

It was during 314 AD when a civil war broke out between Licinius I and Constantine I. The intent to rule by himself led Constantine to use the pretext that Licinius was harboring a fugitive accused of plotting to overthrow him. In the end, Constantine I the Great had Licinius hung, accusing him of conspiring to raise troops among the barbarians. His son, Licinius II, was also executed.

Alexander of Carthage. Usurper (308-310AD)
Æ Follis (4.57 grams) Carthage Mint
Aquila between standards RIC 72

Next, we come to Alexander of Carthage (308-310 AD) who saw an opportunity for power. He was the Prefect of Africa who led a revolt in 308 AD against the tyranny of the Italian usurper Maxentius (306-312 AD) in North Africa. Maxentius's position was unanimously declared illegal by the Tetrarchy, and they declared him to be a public enemy. Maxentius's territory was bordered by the territories of Constantine I the Great and Licinius. The illegal status of Maxentius gave hope to the outlying provinces to stage a rebellion of their own against Rome, where Maxentius had taken control.

The North Africans had been attached to Maxentius only because of their loyalty to Maximianus, and once the rift occurred between father and son, they quickly set up their own Emperor, L. Domitius Alexander (308-310 AD). The usurper was able to maintain his independence for about three years and even entered into alliance negotiations with Constantine. Hence, we see once again the design symbolizing civil war of the legionary eagle standard (aquila) between two legionary standards (signa or vexilla).

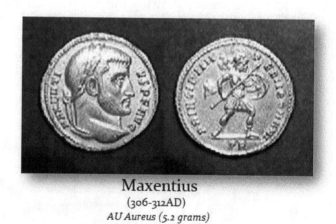

Maxentius
(306-312AD)
AU Aureus (5.2 grams)

Antony struck many millions of his legionary denarii, and they would have been well-known in their day. Thus, they symbolize, on one hand, the end of the Republic and the birth of Imperial Rome and the Battle of Actium.

Conclusion

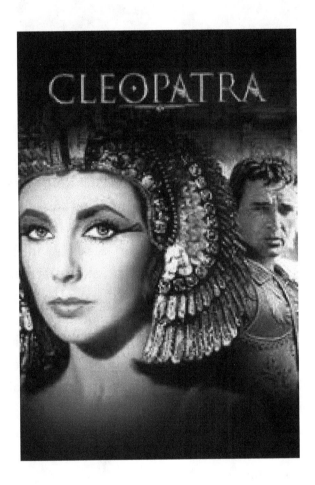

THE NONSENSE THAT Cleopatra was Black is a perverted woke desire to rewrite history. Such perversions alter the entire story of Cleopatra, reducing her to a lovesick fool. This recasting of historical events as an interracial love affair, rather than a calculated proxy way to conquer Rome, hides the talent, motivation, and capability of Cleopatra.

Cleopatra VII's goal was to reestablish the Macedonian kingdom of Alexander the Great. She was an inbred queen, as was the tradition of the Ptolemy dynasty, not to mention the common practice in Egypt at the time. After all, Ptolemy II Philadelphos meant brotherly love in the incestuous context. I seriously doubt that an African would have cared so much about Greece. Additionally, she was not madly in love with Mark Antony as a lovesick fool. Some people love romantic stories of finding that one person to spend life with till the end. That may sell movies, yet once again it is romantic revision of history that Netflix seemed to embrace in this new world of wokeism.

Cleopatra VII (51–30BC)
Alexandria, Egypt Æ 80 Drachmae

Cleopatra VII knew her place in history. She was determined, cunning, and highly intelligent. She did not seek wealth or blissful sex; it was power and evening the score to restore the glory of the Greek empire of Alexander the Great. None of her coinage or surviving busts raise the slightest hint of being a Black African to satisfy this woke agenda.

She spoke five languages and was said to have been "dazzlingly intelligent." None of her many issues of coins show any such trait of being a Black African. That fiction takes away from her true motives and reduces her to some sex-crazed woman void of any real objectives in life.

Cleopatra VII was simply a very proud Greek who was motivated by the fact that the Romans had conquered the known world that they created. After all, it was Alexander the Great who introduced coinage to Egypt. They never even issued their own coinage before the Greek conquest.

That was her motive: to restore the glory that was Macedonia once again. The glory of Philip II in conquering all of Greece, his assassination, and then his dream of conquering the known world was carried out by his son Alexander the Great. Yet it is also Alexander who established the very first one-world currency. He created mints around the world, and they all struck coins with the same motif, but with a mintmark to identify the mint.

Macedonian Kingdom. Alexander III the Great
AR Silver Tetradrachm (17.21 g) struck 325-323/2BC Amphipolis Mint

Cleopatra, through her actions, sought to manipulate Pompey Jr., then Julius Caesar, and finally Mark Antony, to gain control over Rome. Her goal was always the same—the conquest of Rome for the glory of Macedonia. She knew how to manipulate men and used her beauty, sex appeal, and intellect to conquer Rome, using its own troops to do her bidding. This was Cleopatra's proxy war no different than the United States using Ukraine to attack Russia.

Philip II (b 382BC; 360-336BC) of Macedonia

Silver Tetradrachm
(14.4 grams)

Cleopatra Selene
(40– c. 5 BC)

Cleopatra and Antony were survived by their daughter, Cleopatra Selene, who was taken back to Rome when she was ten years old. There she was educated, as was her eventual husband, Juba II. She was placed in the household of Octavian's sister, Octavia the Younger, a former wife of her father, Mark Antony. There she was protected by Octavian/Augustus and eventually married to Juba II of Mauretania to quell the tide of resentment.

Cleopatra VII's daughter inherited her mother's intelligence. She gathered scholars and artists from her mother's royal court in Alexandria to serve in Caesarea when she was married to Juba II. The kingdom of Mauretania was in Algeria. The capital city of Caesarea is known today as Cherchell.

In turn, Cleopatra Selene and Juba II had a son born in 10 BC who they named Ptolemy, keeping in spirit the roots to Macedonia. After his mother died at the age of thirty-five in 5 BC, he ruled Mauretania together with his father, who died in 23 AD.

Cleopatra Æ24 Damascus, Syria

Ptolemy of Mauretania
(circa 20-40AD)
AR Denarius (2.00 grams) Caesarea mint
Son of Cleopatra Selene - Grandson of Mark Antony & Cleopatra VII

Agrippina, Sr
daughter of Agrippa & Julia

ArmstrongEconomics.COM

Ptolemy of Mauretania was therefore the grandson of Mark Antony. However, he was the last of the bloodline of the Macedonian heirs of Ptolemy. Thus, he would formally be the end of the heirs from Alexander the Great.

Ptolemy reigned until 40 AD, until Emperor Caligula (37-41 AD) took the throne of Rome. Caligula's mother, Agrippina the Elder, was the daughter of Marcus Agrippa and Augustus's daughter, Julia the Elder, who was banished by her father for her promiscuous behavior in Rome.

Antonia Junior (36 BC-37 AD) was the younger of two surviving daughters of Mark Antony and Octavia and thus was the niece of Emperor Augustus. This made her also the paternal grandmother of Emperor Caligula, which through Mark Antony meant that there was a blood connection also to Ptolemy.

Antonia - Younger Daughter of Mark Antony & Octavia
(36BC - 37 AD)
AR Denarius Bust rt/Constantiae Augusti Cerces Standing with torch & cornucopiae
ArmstrongEconomics.COM

{}

Gaius (Caligula) (37-41AD)
Æ Sestertius (36mm, 28.31 grams) Rome mint Struck 37-38AD
Laureate head left / addressing troops RIC I 32

ArmstrongEconomics.COM

It has long been debated as to why Caligula made the decision to execute Ptolemy of Mauretania. He may have simply been consumed with jealousy that the people cheered Ptolemy and his roots to Mark Antony. Suetonius tells us that Ptolemy went to visit Rome, where he was declared to be a "friend and ally." Caligula took Ptolemy to the Circus Maximus where, being an independent king, he was allowed to wear purple, a color reserved for kings or the emperor. The people cheered Ptolemy and the admiration of the people quite possibly stirred the jealousy inside Caligula who thought he was also a god. This was the year 40 AD, when the insanity of Caligula and personal depravity, along with his oppression of the Senate, had become too much.

Additionally, there are theories that political or economic reasons may have motivated Caligula. He spent extravagantly, along with precious gem-studded yachts. Apparently, he steadily drained the treasury by some three billion sestertii, an amount which had been left to him by Tiberius. As Caligula discovered the exhausted state of his treasury, his generosity turned into punitive taxation, extortion, and confiscation of private assets. Mauretania certainly offered a pile of wealth.

Claudius
(41 - 54AD)
"SC" SENATUS CONSULTUS (issued by the Senate)
Æ Bronze As

ArmstrongEconomics.COM

Emperor Claudius (41-54 AD) assumed control of Mauretania since the bloodline died with Ptolemy. That is when the kingdom became a Roman province and the Macedonian inheritance of the empire of Alexander the Great formally died. Cleopatra's dream also died a sound death with Ptolemy.

Battle of Issus, November 333BC, Alexander v Persian King Darius
Roman Copy of a lost Alexander Mosaic, c. 100BC
from the House of the Faun, Pompeii

Legion CHORTIS SPECVLATORVM

Mark Antony

Battle of Actium September 2, 31BC
CHORTIS • SPECVLATORVM
Three signa decorated with wreaths and rostra
AR Denarius (3.79 grams) Crawford 544/12

T HE LEGIONARY DENARII struck *Cohortis Speculatorum* ("Cohort of Scouts"), was for the ancient version of what we would call today the CIA (Central Intelligence Agency). Every legion under the Roman Republic at this period would typically have 10 speculatores who served as the legion's intelligence officers. They gathered intelligence by scouting ahead of the legion, as well as carrying messages, and acted as spies.

Antony expanded this function by creating a special *Cohortis Speculatorum* and he struck special "legionary denarii" for them, as well.

The reverse of the denarius minted for the speculatores differed from that of the standard legionary denarius in both design and inscription. Take notice that the inscription referred to the CHORTIS SPECVLATRORVM rather than a legion, and instead of displaying an aquila standing between two signa, these coins presented three signa, each of which had two wreaths and a miniature galley prow.

The wreaths on the signa most likely referred to some victory that was won due to their specific efforts of this intelligence unit.

The denarii of the *Cohort of Speculators* are a more common than those issued for the Praetorian Cohort.

Legion CHORTIVM PRAETORIARVM

Mark Antony
Battle of Actium September 2, 31BC
CHORTIVM PRAETORIARVM
Aquila between two standards
AR Denarius (3.59 grams) Crawford 544/8

EVEN BEFORE THERE were emperors, Roman Republican generals were always accompanied by their elite bodyguard units known as praetorian cohorts (guard). They took their name from *praetorium* meaning the "general's tent" and *cohortis* meaning "cohort," which was a military unit within a legion that consisted of six *centuriae*. A "century" was a sub-unit of a legion that originally consisted of 100 men and came from the Latin *centum*, meaning hundred. This unit was then led by a centurion, its commander. However, just as inflation takes place, here at this late stage in the Republic, what was 100 men has dwindled down to just about eighty men. The *praetorian cohorts* eventually evolved into the Praetorian Guard of the Roman emperors.

Going into the Battle of Actium, Antony's would have had at least four praetorian cohorts. Therefore, the coinage struck for the Praetorian Guard was certainly fewer than those for a legion. Antony's praetorian cohorts would not have been part of a legion, for they were his separate bodyguard. Look closely and you will see that these coins make no mention of any specific legion. They were simply an elite body with the function of protecting Antony.

This is why the issued coins for this elite group only state CHORTIVM PRAETORIARVM yet note that the two standards and aquila in the center is the basic design for the legionary denarii.

Legion Prima Denarius

Mark Antony
Battle of Actium September 2, 31BC
LEG PRI Aquila between two standards
AR Denarius - Crawford 544/13

O F ALL THE legionary denarii of Mark Antony, the debate over the authenticity of Legion PRI (first) has raged on for decades, particularly since there were none discovered in the 1905 Delos Hoard containing 604 coins. This legion I was probably founded in 48 BC by Julius Caesar during the civil war against Pompey. It saw its first action at Dyrrhachium (Spring 48). It acquired the name Germanica since it later served during the Germanic wars.

The design is the same as the legionary issues with the praetorian galley on the obverse and the legend inscription which read:

ANT•AVG III•VIR•R•P•C

This legend is *Antonii Auguris Tresviri Rei Publicae Constituendae* meaning "of Antony, the Augur and One of the Triumvirs for Organizing the Republic." The title "Augur" means that Antony is a priest in the Roman state religion. He is still referring to himself as a "Triumvir" as he is a member of the former Second Triumvirate. It is interesting that here we have as part of the legend inscription "AVG" that would later be used on the coinage to infer that he is the head of state—Augustus.

Turning to the reverse we find the depiction of an *aquila* between two *signa*, the standards for smaller units within a legion. The inscription is LEG PRI (First Legion: *Legio Prima*) identifies this as the first legion and the standard design of the aquila between the two standards adopted by Antony suggesting civil war.

Mark Antony
Battle of Actium September 2, 31BC
LEG PRI Aquila between two standards
AR Denarius (3.37 grams) Crawford 544/13
The Tardani counterfeit

Legio Prima Denarius – Fake

For whatever reason, the rarity of this First Legion has often been considered to imply that those which exist under Antony are simply counterfeit. Pictured here is a highly deceptive forgery created by the Italian forger Tardani who seems to have worked in Rome from the 1890s up until about World War I. His main area of forgeries was medieval Italian coins, where his forgeries of papal coinage remain extremely deceptive.

However, Tardani also produced some ancient forgeries as well as early French Carolingian coinage. They are of exceptionally high-quality, using examples that he seems to have taken from reference books. Over 1,000 of his dies were finally acquired in 1919 after his death by the Museo Nazionale Romano. Some also exist in the Smithsonian.

Legion II Denarius

Mark Antony
Battle of Actium September 2, 31BC
LEG II Aquila between two standards
AR Denarius (3.96 grams) Crawford 544/14

MANY HAVE ARGUED that the Antonian legionary series begins with LEG II, which was the most common coin discovered in the 1905 Delos Hoard —forty in all. Known as Legio II Sabina (Sabine), its early name was the Legio II Augusta. Many consider this to be the first actual legionary denarius issued by Antony and Cleopatra.

Antony is identified as the issuer of this series by name and his titles:

ANT AVG III VIR R.P.C

Abbreviating Antonii, auguris, tresviri rei publicae constituendae ("Antony, Augur, and Triumvir for the Organizing of the Republic")

Therefore, most consider that there were only twenty-two legions (Legiones II - XXIII) along with their numerals, LEG XII ANTIQVAE ("venerable"), LEG XVII CLASSICAE ("of the fleet"), and LEG XVIII LYBICAE ("Lybian"). Yet there have been other legions that have surfaced which are genuine and were part of the whole propaganda effort.

Several legionary numerals are also rendered in different forms (i.e. IV and IIII, IX and VIIII, XIX and XVIIII). Thus, the actual varieties far outnumber the legions represented. Two specialized units also receive coins: The Praetorian Cohorts, Antony's personal guard, and the speculatores, or scouts, with the latter signified by specially decorated naval standards.

The silver content was about 92% fine, which was a slight debasement from the standard 96% fine standard at this point in time. Because of the sheer volume of coins that have existed, it would imply that his troops' strength was perhaps at least 200,000, all funded by Cleopatra.

Legion III Denarius

Mark Antony
Battle of Actium September 2, 31BC
LEG III Aquila between two standards
AR Denarius (3.37 grams) Crawford 544/15

THIS LEGION WAS probably the legion that appears in the historical record as Legion III Gallica, a legion that Julius Caesar raised during his campaigns in Gaul and participated in the civil war against Pompey. Antony took over this legion after Caesar's death. It is possible that Antony may have raised an entirely new Legion III from North Africa.

Legio III, later named Gallica ("from Gaul"), was raised by Julius Caesar in 49 BC and fought subsequently in the civil wars of the late republic. After Actium, it was taken over by Octavian and went on to a lengthy career under the empire, mainly stationed in Syria, where it was recorded until the mid-third century AD, after which its history becomes obscure.

When we look at the Delos hoard, there were twenty-five specimens of Legion III compared to forty for Legion II. Therefore, this was not one of the rarest legionary denarii to have survived.

Legion IV Denarius

Mark Antony
Battle of Actium September 2, 31BC
LEG IV Aquila between two standards
AR Denarius (3.57 grams) Crawford 544/17

THE LEGION IV denarius is one of the more common with twenty-eight contained in the Delos hoard of 1905. Still, they will command a good premium in high quality as most legionary denarii. The background of Legion IV reflects that it later came to be known as Legion IV Scythica and was most likely a legion Antony had originally raised for his campaign against the Parthians, also known as Legion IV Parthica.

The legion also has the much rarer version of IIII of where there were none found in the Delos hoard. Nevertheless, Legion IV in high grades will bring about the same price as an ounce of gold: more than $2,000.

Legion IIII Denarius

Mark Antony

Battle of Actium September 2, 31BC
LEG IIII Aquila between two standards
AR Denarius (3.44 grams) Crawford 544/16

THERE IS AN extremely rare variety of Legion IV whereby the Legion IV is written as LEG IIII. The Legion IIII denarius is without question extremely rare. There were none discovered in the 1905 Delos Hoard.

Very few examples exist. Most are worn and certainly not in high grade. The collector waiting for an EF specimen will most likely die before ever completing this series. I have found only three specimens that I could document, and nothing exists whatsoever in any high grade.

As mentioned previously, legionary denarii circulated for decades. This is why the few surviving examples I have encountered are usually highly worn or have other problems of flat strike. Crawford lists this variety as 544/16.

Legion V Denarius

Mark Antony
Battle of Actium September 2, 31BC
LEG V Aquila between two standards
AR Denarius (3.76 grams) Crawford 544/18

Antony's Legion V may have been the famous Legion V *Alaudae* ("the larks"). They were a Caesarean legion that remained loyal to Antony for the Battle of Actium. Others have suggested that this may have been Legion V Macedonica, a Caesarean legion about which we know next to nothing. Still there are others who have suggested it was Legion V Urbana, a legion raises

by Antony, which was disbanded after Actium. Still others suggest that it was Legion V Gallica, a Caesarean legion that lost its legionary eagle to German raiders in Gaul in 17 BC.

Legion V was the second most common legion discovered in the 1905 Delos Hoard. In total, there were thirty-seven specimens with the most common being Legion II with forty examples out of 604.

Legion VI Denarius

Mark Antony

Battle of Actium September 2, 31BC
LEG VI Aquila between two standards
AR Denarius (3.68 grams) Crawford 544/19

L EGION VI WAS founded originally by Julius Caesar in 52 BC during his conquest of Gaul (59-49 BC). The VI became one of his most reliable legions and was with Caesar when he crossed the Rubicon and confronted the corrupt Senate. Indeed, the coins minted by Caesar to pay his troops depicted the elephant crushing the snake, which was the corrupt Senate led by Cato.

The Legion VI also stood by Caesar at the battles of Alexandria in Egypt and Zela in modern-day Turkey in Asia Minor. It was that battle where Caesar uttered his famous saying "veni, vidi, vici"—"I came, I saw, I conquered."

PADUAN Sesterius Medalian (VENI-VIDI-VICI)

Legion VI denarii of Antony are the third most common in the 1905 Delos Hoard with thirty-six specimens out of 604. Once again, high grade examples will bring the equivalent of slightly more than one ounce of gold.

After Caesar, Legion VI eventually became Legio VI Ferrata ("Ironsides") and was under the command of Mark Antony after Caesar's assassination.

Around 40 BC, Octavian raised his own Legio VI, perhaps using a core of veterans from Caesar's original legion. Legio VI fought with Octavian at Perusia in 41 BC against Mark Antony's wife Fulvia and Lucius Antonius in the Pannonian campaigns of 39-36 AD, and later at Actium.

Mark Antony & Lucius Antonius
AV Aureus
ArmstrongEconomics.COM

After Actium, Octavian (later Augustus) stationed his Legio VI in Spain. Augustus and Agrippa led the VI to victory over the Cantabrians between 25 and 13 BC.

Legion VII Denarius

Mark Antony
Battle of Actium September 2, 31BC
LEG VII Aquila between two standards
AR Denarius (3.76 grams) Crawford 544/20

Antony's Legion VII denarii were represented in the 1905 Delos Hoard with twenty-seven specimens recorded. We are not certain if Antony raised his own Legion VII. We do know that in 36 BC, veterans settled in southern Gaul. The Legio VII was first raised in 65 BC in Spain by Pompey the Great. However, after 58 BC, it served under Julius Caesar in his Gallic Wars (58-50 BC). Legion VII was one of two legions that Caesar took with him when he first invaded Britain.

There was a legion VII that was with Octavian during his war against Sextus Pompeius. It is not clear if this same Legion VII was with Octavian at the Battle of Actium in 31 BC.

Legion VIII Denarius

Mark Antony
Battle of Actium September 2, 31BC
LEG VIII Aquila between two standards
AR Denarius (3.78 grams) Crawford 544/21

L EGION VIII AUGUSTA was one of the oldest legions of the Imperial Roman army. There were twenty-seven specimens in the 1905 Delos Hoard out of 604. This legion was under Julius Caesar during the Gallic Wars. This legion was also part of the Cisalpine Gaul action around 58 BC when Caesar moved to address a widespread revolt in Gaul (modern-day France). Caesar moved against the rebellion to pacify the unruly tribes of the region.

Six years into the invasion, in 52 AD, Vercingetorix of the Arverni led a second insurrection and rallied together many tribes.

CR 448/2a
Vercingetorix (82-46 BC) Gallic chieftain

Battle of Alesia

It was the VIII Legion that stood by Caesar throughout the Gallic Wars and participated in the famous Battle of Alesia in 52 BC. Julius Caesar laid siege to Alesia, where Gallic general Vercingetorix and his massive host were residing. Caesar directed his troops to erect a series of extensive fortifications, including two walls encircling the city, to keep the defenders in and potential reinforcements out. Indeed, Caesar proved to be an expert strategist and always wore his red cloak, so everyone knew where he was during a battle.

Despite fending off reinforcements and surrounding Vercingetorix, finally his resistance collapsed and eventually he surrendered. This marked the final major military engagement of the Gallic Wars, securing Roman authority over Gaul in its entirety and this created the civilizing of Europe.

Legion VII was given the title "Gallica" for its steadfast position during the Battle of Alesia. They were with Caesar at the Battle of Pharsalus. Later, they were with Caesar in Egypt when he restored Cleopatra to the throne. In 46 BC, this legion also fought in the Battle of Thapsus in modern-day Tunisia before it was disbanded.

After Caesar's assassination, this legion was with Mark Antony against Decimus Brutus, where it earned the nickname "Mutinensis."

Legion IIX Denarius

Mark Antony
Battle of Actium September 2, 31BC
LEG IIX Aquila between two standards
AR Denarius (3.98 grams) Crawford 544/22
Extremely Rare

HERE WE HAVE Legion Eight but written IIX instead of VIII. There were none of these found in the 1905 Delos Hoard. Crawford lists that this Legion VIII also has a variety written as "LEG IIX" but does not list them separately. This is probably the rarest of the legionary denarii. While I personally have never seen such a denarius, nor have any showed up for sale that I have been able to find in the last twenty years, I am told that three examples have existed.

Legion IIX is not reference in the seminal work of Michael Crawford, *Roman Republican Coinage*, neither in the main text nor in appendix page 552. A reliable friend saw a worn example in trade about twenty years ago with an old patina, in normal style and not hyped up as anything special. NAC also sold an example in 2008 Auction 45, lot 59, which was the ex-Barry Feirstein collection, which brought only 5'750CHF.

59

59   *Marcus Antonius.* Denarius, mint moving with Mark Antony (Patrae ?) 32-31, AR 3.65 g. ANT AVG · III·
VIR·R·P·C Galley r., with sceptre tied with fillet on prow. Rev. LEG – IIX *Aquila* between two standards.
B. Antonia –. C –. Sydenham –. Seaby 35a. Sear Imperators 358 note. Crawford 544/21.
        Of the highest rarity, apparently only the second specimen known. Metal somewhat
                                        porous, otherwise about extremely fine   2'500
Privately purchased from Harlan J. Berk.

Mark Antony struck his 'legionary' coinage in vast quantities as he and his wife, the Egyptian queen Cleopatra VII,
prepared for war with Octavian and his commander Marcus Agrippa. In the end, their efforts were futile: Antony and
Cleopatra fled the battle at Actium on September 2, 31 B.C. once they realized they would not win the day. Antony was
murdered when he disembarked at Alexandria and Cleopatra, who had arrived safely, chose suicide over becoming the
trophy of Octavian's triumph.
Twenty-three legions are celebrated on Antony's 'legionary' coinage by their number, and two are identified by their name
(the cohort of *speculatores* and the praetorian cohorts). Of the numbered legions, most are indicated simply by Roman
numerals, while three of those legions are honoured with a supplementary issue that provides their honorific title: XII
Antiqvae, XVII *Classicae* and XVIII *Lybicae*. Perhaps the most famous rarity in this regard is the issue for Legion I, which
is rendered LEG PRI.
This coin is of particular interest because of the unusual form of its inscription, which provides the number for the eighth
legion as IIX rather than the common form VIII. The other examples of duplication of legionary numbers include the fourth
(IIII and IV), the ninth (VIIII and IX), the fourteenth (XIII and XIV) and the nineteenth (XVIII and XIX). In each of these
four cases, however, the numbers of the legions are one numeral beneath a five or a zero; the same cannot be said for the
present coin, which is two numerals beneath, and thus is an unexpected rendering.

    This is the detail of the Barry Feirstein specimen, and appears to be a genuine example, confirming
that the engraver, perhaps bored, engraved the die IIX instead of VIII.[5]

---

5   https://www.arsclassicacoins.com/wp-content-nasecure/uploads/2020/06/2008-NAC-45.pdf

This example appeared in a Gorny sale in 2015. It appears to be fake because the lettering is clearly inconsistent with the entire series.[6]

H.A. Seaby 1967 Roman Silver Coins

Legion IIX is mentioned in *Roman Silver Coins*, 1978, vol.1 page 124, number 35a, without citing a source. It is NOT mentioned in *Roman Silver Coins* vol.1, 1952 edition or the 1967 edition. Herbert Allen Seaby (1898-1979), author of that reference, handled an example sometime between 1967 and 1978 and then added it to his catalogue.

Consequently, there are three known examples that have passed through the trade, the Seaby post 1967s, the Feirstein coin, and the one I saw, and that the type is authentic.

---

6   https://www.acsearch.info/search.html?id=3384757

Legion VIIII Denarius

Mark Antony
Battle of Actium September 2, 31BC
LEG VIIII Aquila between two standards
AR Denarius (4.04 grams) Crawford 544/22

LEGION VIIII (9) is one of the more difficult of the legionary denarii of Mark Antony to obtain. There were fifteen in the 1905 Delos Hoard. This is not to be confused with a similar legion under the command of Octavian. This is the Antony's Legion, which was disbanded or incorporated into another legion after Actium.

This Legion was also represented with Roman numerals IX which was a little more common in the 1905 Delos Hoard with twenty specimens v fifteen of the VIIII, which was Known as Legio VIIII Hispana, or in other words, "the Spanish Legion" recruited from that province.

Legion IX Denarius

Mark Antony
Battle of Actium September 2, 31BC
LEG IX Aquila between two standards
AR Denarius (3.85 grams) Crawford 544/23

THE FABLED NINTH Legion vanished from the historical record which has sparked a long-winded debate for centuries. This has been a historical mystery from the Roman period whereby this legion disappeared from history sometime after 120 AD.

Nevertheless, Mark Antony and Cleopatra produced denarii for Legion IX and there were twenty specimens found in the 1905 Delos Hoard. Legio IX Hispana was recorded as active during the first century BC and was engaged in the Social War, also called the Italian, or Marsic War.

The legion was then incorporated into the forces commanded by Julius Caesar during the Gallic Wars, and the subsequent Civil War. It was recalled by Octavian against Sextus Pompey.

Antony's Legio IX was either disbanded or absorbed into Octavian's after the Battle of Actium.

Legion X Denarius

Mark Antony
Battle of Actium September 2, 31BC
LEG X Aquila between two standards
AR Denarius (4.12 grams) Crawford 544/24
Scarce Legion

O F ALL THE Roman legions, Legio X is the most famous since it was the favorite of Julius Caesar in Gaul and was often his personal bodyguard. Antony's Legio X proved so loyal to him that Octavian disbanded the unit and replaced it with his own Legio X Gemina (twin).

When we look at the 1905 Delos Hoard, there were twenty-eight specimens out of 604. That was about half of one percent.

Legion XI Denarius

Mark Antony
Battle of Actium September 2, 31BC
LEG XI Aquila between two standards
AR Denarius (3.78 grams) Crawford 544/25

Antony's Legion XI was represented in the Delos Hoard by twenty-four specimens. Because of the sheer volume of coins that were being minted, it is quite common to see uneven strike and designs that are off-center.

This legion was known as Legio XI Claudia between 58–45 BC. Its emblem was that of Neptune. It has been disbanded after the civil war. However, it was recalled by Augustus to fight after the assassins.

LEG XI

Legion XII Denarii

Mark Antony
Battle of Actium September 2, 31BC
LEG XII Aquila between two standards
AR Denarius (3.74 grams) Crawford 544/26

THE TWELFTH LEGION was recruited by the Julius Caesar for his campaign against the Helvetians (Swiss) in 58 BC. Following the Civil War, Caesar bestowed the title *Victrix* (Victorious) upon this legion. It was recalled after Caesar's assassination by Lepidus in 44 BC. Thereafter, Lepidus turned Legion XII over to Mark Antony, which they then stood by in his battle against Octavian.

This legion fought in Antony's ill-fated conquest of Parthia. When Antony was defeated in the naval battle off Actium in 31 BC, some veterans were settled at Patras (in Greece).

Referring once again to the 1905 Delos Hoard, there were twenty-eight specimens that were found.

Legion XII Antiqvae Denarii

Mark Antony

Battle of Actium September 2, 31BC
LEG LEG XII · ANTIQVAE Aquila between two standards
AR Denarius (3.74 grams) Crawford 544/9

THERE ARE TWO major versions of the Legio XII denarius, which together involve long-standing mystery. The standard version is obviously just Legio XII, while the second identifies it as Legio XII Antiqvae (meaning the "ancient one"). The confusion arises from the fact that we also know that Antony led a Legio XII Fulminata ("Thunderbolt"), which was originally raised by Julius Caesar. Antony never issued any denarii with the title "Fulminata." There is no record whatsoever of any such Legio XII Antiquae other than Antony's coinage.

There were only five specimens in the 1905 Delos Hoard, ranking this issue among the rarest to be found.

Legion XIII Denarii

Mark Antony
Battle of Actium September 2, 31BC
LEG LEG XIII Aquila between two standards
AR Denarius (3.66 grams) Crawford 544/27

L EGIO XIII IS one of the most famous Roman legions. Once again, this legion stood by Julius Caesar from its founding circa 57 BC. In 49 BC, this legion crossed the Rubicon River with Caesar in northern Italy, setting off the Civil War that led to the termination of the corrupt Roman Republic.

Antony's thirteenth legion was built around a core of veterans from Caesar's unit. Octavian absorbed it after Actium to form his Legio XIII Gemina of imperial fame.

Looking at the 1905 Delos Hoard, there were twenty specimens found, or about 0.5% of the hoard.

Legion XIV Denarii

Mark Antony
Battle of Actium September 2, 31BC
LEG LEG XIV Aquila between two standards
AR Denarius (3.85 grams) Crawford 544/29

Legio XIV Gemina was formed by Julius Caesar for his campaign in Gaul in 58 BC It remained with him for the Civil War into 58 BC.

Legio XIIII Gemina was disbanded after the Battle of Actium. The veterans of Actium were settled at Ateste in Italy.

The coinage of Legion XIV is rather scarce. There were only twelve specimens found in the 1905 Delos Hoard. Many examples remain poorly struck and off-center.

Legion XIIII Denarii

Mark Antony
Battle of Actium September 2, 31BC
LEG LEG XIIII Aquila between two standards
AR Denarius (3.75 grams) Crawford 544/28

THERE ARE TWO versions of Antony's fourteenth legion—XIIII and XIV. This former version is one of the rarest of the series. There were only six specimens in the 1905 Delos Hoard. Yet is believed that this legion was first recruited by Julius Caesar in 57 BC to fight in Gaul and was wiped out by the Belgian Eburones in early 53 BC. It was reconstituted for the siege of Alesia in 52 BC.

The fourteenth then fought for Caesar against Pompey during the Civil War. It was perhaps used initially by Octavian against Sextus Pompeius's occupation of Sicily. Fourteenth was reinforced with soldiers from the disbanded legions of Mark Antony after the Battle of Actium.

Legion XV Denarii

Mark Antony
Battle of Actium September 2, 31BC
LEG LEG XV Aquila between two standards
AR Denarius (3.79 grams) Crawford 544/30

THE DENARII OF Legion XV are one of the more common legions. There were thirty-nine specimens found in the 1905 Delos Hoard. The Fifteenth Legion was probably originally recruited in 53 BC by Julius Caesar and fought in Gaul. It was transferred to the Senate in 50 BC and stationed in Aquileia. However, when Caesar crossed the Rubicon, the Fifteenth Legion sided with Caesar, knowing full well how corrupt the Senate had become. It went thereafter to occupy North Africa, but it was destroyed in the autumn of 49/48 BC.

The Fifteenth Legion was re-formed by 41 BC and took the name Apollinaris after Apollo. Octavian perhaps chose the surname Apollinaris because he worshipped Apollo above all other gods. He used this legion against Sextus Pompeius's occupation of Sicily.

After Pompey was defeated in 36 BC, the Fifteenth may have then taken the side of Mark Antony for the Battle of Actium. Afterwards, the veterans settled at Ateste, and the Fifteenth was sent to Illyricum, where it stayed for almost forty years.

Legion XVI Denarii

Mark Antony
Battle of Actium September 2, 31BC
LEG LEG XVI Aquila between two standards
AR Denarius (3.67 grams) Crawford 544/31

ANTONY'S SIXTEENTH LEGION denarii in the 1905 Delos Hoard amounted to twenty-four coins. This legion was founded in 41 BC or 40 BC by Julius Caesar's heir Octavian, who needed it to defeat Sextus Pompeius's occupation of Sicily. Pompey was defeated in 36 BC and thereafter this legion was most likely sent to Africa where Antony's XVI coins were found at the site.

The fact that Legion XVI coins have been discovered in North Africa implies that they may have switched sides and joined Mark Antony. Thereafter, Legion XVI was sent to the Rhine to defend against the Germanic hordes. In September 9 AD, it was the XVII, XVIII, and XIX that were annihilated in the Teutoburg Forest Battle. That left the Sixteenth as the only legion preventing a Germanic attack on Gallia Belgica.

Legion XVII Denarii

Mark Antony
Battle of Actium September 2, 31BC
LEG LEG XVII Aquila between two standards
AR Denarius (3.83 grams) Crawford 544/32

Antony's Seventeenth Legion (Legio XVII) was one of the legions wiped out in the famous Battle of Teutoburg Forest in September 9 AD[7] along with the Eighteenth and Nineteenth. We do not know the surname of this legion. It may have been Gallica or Germanica.

Seventeenth is unknown from surviving accounts. It has long been one of the legions that remain a mystery, falling through the cracks of time and circumstance. We do know that Augustus had legions numbered one to twenty-two.

There were three legions lost in the Battle of Teutoburg Forest, and we have confirmation those included the Eighteenth and Nineteenth. The possibility that the Seventeenth was the third legion makes sense since it appears to vanish from history at this point. Moreover, there was a Seventeenth during the civil war between Caesar and Pompey 49-48 BC.

---

7   See Nineteenth for details

After the defeat of Sextus Pompey, that is when Octavian and Antony split.

The legions of the Augustan army were numbered from one to twenty-two. It would not make sense if there had been no such Seventeenth legion.

Antony issued two types with the legend XVII—the Seventeenth. We have this version with just XVII and then we have XXVII Classica ("naval"). Why there are two versions of the Seventeenth is not clear. However, we cannot rule out that Antony was also engaged in propaganda to make his forces appear overwhelming.

The legionary emblem of the Seventeenth is also not known. However, Seventeen may have been retired and never used again after the Battle of Teutoburg Forest.

Legion XVII CLASSICAE

Mark Antony
Battle of Actium September 2, 31BC
LEG LEG XVII CLASSICAE Aquila between two standards
AR Denarius (3.87 grams) Crawford 544/10

THE SEVENTEENTH CLASSICAE (Legio XVII Classicae) means "of the fleet," implying that this is a naval unit. Antony raised Legio XVII Classicae to serve as what might today be a marine unit: *classicae* does not derive from the Latin word meaning "classic," but rather from *classis*, the Latin word for a "naval fleet."

Therefore, this distinction "classicae" meaning "of the fleet," constituted men who were specialized to serve as marines in the coming battle. This only adds to the confusion since they remained ashore during the naval battle of Actium. The Seventeenth legion surrendered to Octavian after the battle.

There is little doubt that Octavian also had his own Seventeenth Legion, and he either disbanded Antony's Seventeenth Legion after the Battle of Actium, or he transferred its surviving legionaries into other units. Octavian's Seventeenth survived the Battle of Actium and went on to serve in Germania until it was wiped out at the Battle of the Teutoburg Forest in September 9 AD.

The Legio XVII Classicae denarius is scarce. There were only eight examples in the 1905 Delos hoard. However, I have seen over sixty specimens sold since about 1997.

Nevertheless, well-centered and high grades are more difficult to come by, but not at the top of the list of rarities.

Legion XVIII Denarii

Mark Antony
Battle of Actium September 2, 31BC
LEG LEG XVIII Aquila between two standards
AR Denarius (4.003 grams) Crawford 544/33

ANTONY'S EIGHTEENTH LEGION (Legio XVIII) may have been known as Gallica, or Germanica. On this point, we cannot be certain. The Eighteenth is one of the three legions wiped out in the famous Battle of Teutoburg Forest in September 9 AD, along with the Seventeenth and Nineteenth.

There is a record of the Eighteenth fighting under a governor named Gaius Cornelius Lentulus Spinther in 56-53 BC in Cilicia, which was located in southern Anatolia (modern-day Turkey) bordering Persia (Iran) and Syria.

During the civil war between Caesar and Pompey the Great in 49-48 BC, both had legions with these numbers. We do not know what happened to these legions after the civil war. There is a tombstone of an officer who served in the Eighteenth Legion located in the Museo Nazionale Romano.

Consequently, Antony's Eighteenth legion of Lybica may be this historical legion. It may have been one created by Antony to further his propaganda agenda.

The Eighteenth was sent to the Rhine about 15 AD, together with Sixteenth Gallica and the Seventeenth legion. After the conquest in the region led by Augustus's generals Drusus (13 BC -9 AD) and Tiberius (8 BC- 4-5 AD), Augustus sent Publius Quinctilius Varus to rule the region as a governor and impose taxation.

Legion XIIX Denarii

Mark Antony

Battle of Actium September 2, 31BC
LEG LEG XIIX Aquila between two standards
AR Denarius (3.88 grams) Crawford 544/29

THIS VERSION OF the Eighteenth Legion expressed as LEG XIIX may be the rarest of all versions for this is the only example I have discovered. There were only six Legion XVIII in the 1905 Delos Hoard and this variety did not exist. It was sold in the Vecchi Auction 2 sale of September 1996 for $6,500 and listed as "Extremely Rare."

This appears to be the rarest of all the legionary denarii of Mark Antony issued for the Battle of Actium.

Legion XVIII LYBICAE

Mark Antony
Battle of Actium September 2, 31BC
LEG LEG XVIII LYBICAE Aquila between two standards
AR Denarius (3.74 grams) Crawford 544/11

THERE ARE THREE versions of the legionary denarius Antony struck for his Eighteenth Legion that he raised before the Battle of Actium from Libya. This scarcer version identifies the legion as LEG XVIII *Lybicae* ("from Libya") raised with the help of Cleopatra. The third version is the extremely rare "XIIX" for eighteen. In the 1905 Delos Hoard, there were only four of this version found.

Of the twenty-two legions named on Mark Antony's legionary denarii, only three carried special names along with their numerals, namely: the Legio XII Antiquae, the Legio XVII Classicae, and the Legio XVIII Lybicae. They are distinct and distinguished from Octavian's similarly numbered legions. They were raised on short notice by Antony prior to the Battle of Actium. The name "Lybica" indicates that its soldiers came from Libya. This legion was disbanded in 31 BC by Octavian after the Battle of Actium.

Legion XVIIII Denarii

Mark Antony
Battle of Actium September 2, 31BC
LEG LEG XVIIII Aquila between two standards
AR Denarius (3.75 grams) Crawford 544/34

THE NINETEENTH LEGION of Antony, expressed as XVIIII, is one of the rarest denarii. There were none found in the 1905 Delos Hoard. Nonetheless, it is classified by Crawford as 544/34. The specimen illustrated above was sold for about $25,000 in 2023 at Auction 123 of Classical Numismatic Group lot 565. That was effectively ten ounces of gold at the time.

This was a separate legion freshly raised by Antony prior to the Battle of Actium. Afterwards, Octavian disbanded this legion and merged the men into another legion.

Once again, Antony issues so many denarii that their production must have been a nightmare. Engravers were perhaps bored, inscribing versions of numerals just to make things different.

Legion XIX Denarii

Mark Antony

Battle of Actium September 2, 31BC
LEG LEG XIX Aquila between two standards
AR Denarius (3.9 grams) Crawford 544/35

Tʜᴇ Nɪɴᴇᴛᴇᴇɴᴛʜ Lᴇɢɪᴏɴ (Legio XIX) was the original legion wiped out in the famous battle in the Teutoburg Forest along with the Seventeenth and Eighteenth legions in September 9 AD during the reign of Augustus. Publius Quinctilius Varus (46 BC–9 AD) was a Roman general sent by Augustus to preside in Germany. Varus is remembered for having lost the three Roman legions when they were ambushed by Germanic forces in the Battle of the Teutoburg Forest. Varus then committed suicide.

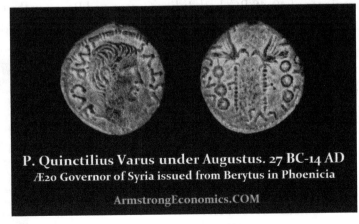

P. Quinctilius Varus under Augustus. 27 BC-14 AD
Æ20 Governor of Syria issued from Berytus in Phoenicia

ArmstrongEconomics.COM

Germanicus (Died 19AD)
AE Dupondius struck by his son Caligula
*Germanicus holding aquila commemorating his recovery of
two of the three eagles lost by Varus in the Teutoburg Forest*

It was Germanicus, father of Caligula (37-41 AD) who recovered two of the three standards that Varus had lost in the Teutoburg Forest battle. In 15 AD, the eagle of the Nineteenth Legion was recovered by the Roman commander Lucius Stertinius among the Bructeri. The legionary emblem of legion XIX is not known.

AUGUSTUS (27BC-14 AD)
Æ As of Lugdunum (Lyon) mint circa 15-10 BC
Countermarked by P. Quinctilius Varus

Interestingly, coins of Augustus minted at Lugdunum (Lyons, France) exist with counterstamps "VAR" by Varus prior to the battle.

The surname of the Nineteenth is not known but may have been Gallica, or Germanica. During the civil war of 49-48 BC, both Julius Caesar and Pompey the Great employed legions with these numbers, but it is not certain if they were disbanded in the aftermath.

The Nineteenth was raised by Mark Antony prior to the Battle of Actium, which his coins proclaim. They may have been disbanded in 31 BC by Octavian, following his victory at the Battle of Actium.

However, it has also been argued that the Nineteenth was founded in 41-40 BC in the aftermath of the Battle of Philippi where the assassins Brutus and Cassius were defeated. Octavian may have raised the Nineteenth when he needed fresh troops to defend against Sextus Pompeius's occupation of Sicily and his blockade of the grain supply of Rome. But this is speculation.

Legion XX Denarii

Mark Antony
Battle of Actium September 2, 31BC
LEG LEG XX Aquila between two standards
AR Denarius (4.02 grams) Crawford 544/36

HERE WE HAVE Antony's Legion XX, which may have been Legio XX Siciliana, originally raised by Octavian in 36 BC to invade Sicily to confront Sextus Pompey. The question becomes was this legion then loyal to Antony?

We also have Legio XX Valeria Victrix which would be normally read as "victorious black eagle." The alternative translation might be read as "valiant and victorious."

Once again, this legion appears to have been absorbed by Octavian in the aftermath of the Battle of Actium in 31 BC. It was re-formed from various survivors of the conflict.

Legion XX Denarii

Mark Antony
Battle of Actium, September, 31 BC
LEG XX, Aquila between two standards
AR Quinarius, Lugdunum? Crawford 544/36

Legion XXI Denarii

Mark Antony
Battle of Actium September 2, 31BC
LEG LEG XXI Aquila between two standards
AR Denarius (3.91 grams) Crawford 544/37

THERE WERE TWENTY-THREE specimens of this Legion XXI in the Delos Hoard which contained 604 legionary denarii. Legio XXI Rapax ("Predator") was a legion thought to have been formally founded in 31 BC after the Battle of Actium, perhaps taking the place of Antony's. That is when it was named Legio XXI Rapax and its symbol became that of Octavian's—the Capricorn.

Therefore, the origin of this number may have indeed been from Antony and Cleopatra. The absorbtion by Octavian after Actium appears to make sense then.

Legion XXII Denarii

Mark Antony
Battle of Actium September 2, 31BC
LEG LEG XXII Aquila between two standards
AR Denarius (3.65 grams) Crawford 544/38

HERE WE HAVE Antony's Legion XXII. There were only fifteen such specimens in the 1905 Delos Hoard. Legio XXII Deiotariana ("Deiotarus") referred to Deiotarus (c. 105–42 BC), the Celtic king of Galatia, in modern Turkey. He was a trusted ally of Caesar and the Romans.

Consequently, Julius Caesar founded this legion of the Imperial Roman army in 48 BC but it was raised by Deiotarus. It survived until it was disbanded during the Jewish Bar Kokhba revolt of 132–136 AD.

Deiotarus raised this legion and trained it with Roman help. It was composed of 12,000 infantrymen and 2,000 horsemen. Cicero tells us that it was divided into thirty cohorts. That would have been the equivalent of three Roman legions. This is the army that supported the Romans in their wars against King Mithridates VI of Pontus. However, it suffered a major defeat against King Pharnaces II of Pontus. The survivors formed but a single legion and marched with Caesar against Pontus at the Battle of Zela (47 BC).

Julius Caesar
(100–44BC)

It is not certain if this is the same legion Mark Antony numbered XXII. After the death of Amyntas in 25 BC, who was Deiotarus's successor, the entire Galatian kingdom was simply absorbed into the Roman Empire.

After the Battle of Actium, Octavian had twenty-one legions. It was the absorption of this Legio XXII Deiotariana that formally received the number XXII.

Legion XXIII Denarii

Mark Antony
Battle of Actium September 2, 31BC
LEG LEG XXIII Aquila between two standards
AR Denarius (3.95 grams) Crawford 544/39

A NTONY'S LEGION XXIII denarii were included in the 1905 Delos Hoard, which contained twenty-four specimens. This is the highest numbered legion at full strength that we can confirm. Denarii with higher numbers were likely genuine yet were not at full strength and were probably produced as part of the propaganda intended to convince Octavian and the Senate that Antony had overwhelming support.

After the Battle of Actium, Octavian either disbanded Antony's Twenty-third Legion or transferred its surviving legionaries into other units. After Octavian became Augustus in 27 BCE, he reorganized the Roman Army into twenty-eight legions, but he only numbered them up to XXII.

Legions XXIV – XXX

In 100 AD, Emperor Trajan (reigned 98-117) raised Legio Ulpia Victrix ("Legion XXX Ulpia Victory") for his Dacian War. Previously, there had been no imperial Roman Legion XXX. Legion XXX Classicae (Naval) 48–41 BC of Julius Caesar (100-44BC) existed during the Civil War with Pompey the Great. Caesar also had:

- Legio XXV Martia (49–42 BC) - lost in 42 BC crossing the Adriatic the War
- Legio XXVIII (47–31 BC)
- Legio XXIX (49–30 BC)

Whether Mark Antony officially recorded legionary denarii of XXIV to XXXIII has remained a major question. The consensus has been that all legion numbers above XXIII are either fake or erroneous.

Legions numbered greater than XXIII have existed. If Antony did issue such coins, it is not likely that he had such legions at full force. The possibility that they were intended solely for propaganda purposes cannot be ruled out.

Nonetheless, since these legionary denarii were an extensive issue, none over Legion XXIII were discovered in the 1905 Delos Hoard. This is why consensus remains that anything over Legion XXIII is likely fake or an engraving error.

These coins were struck entirely for sheer intimidation and propaganda purposes to create shock and awe. This was to impress the Senate that Antony had the support of the legions over Octavian. Antony probably made sure that specimens were sent to the Senate. They would customarily be sent as "donatives," or bribes, to senators.

Crawford in his *Roman Republican Coinage* did not list anything higher than Legion XXIII, which was found in the Delos Hoard. Other resources, like Sydenham's *Roman Republican Coinage*, 1952. p. 196, nos. 1247-1253: XXIV, XXV, XXVI, XXVII, XXVIII, XXIX and XXX notes these legions.

A. Banti and L. Simonetti, in *Corpus Nummorum Romanorum II*, pp. 38-41, no. 102-108 record denarii for legions: LEG XXIV (= Turin, Fava 1964, pl. 19, 3); LEG XXV (= Hamburger sale 32, 1933, 547); LEG XXVI (= Babelon 104); LEG XXVII (Paris, BnF); LEG XXVIII (= Babelon 143); LEG XXIX (= Paris, BnF); LEG XXX (= BMCRR II, pl. 116, 12; Brunacci collection, Santamaria sale 1958, 797 [struck over a denarius of Julius Caesar with P. Sepullius Macer]; Ratto sale 1924, 1392).

The counterfeiter Tardani was prolific in Europe during the late nineteenth to early twentieth centuries. Many of the dies Tardani created are now housed in the Smithsonian. It remains speculation that Tardani may have also created from scratch LEG XXIV–XXX (Syd. 1247-1253), which Sear listed as "doubtful" in *Roman Silver Coins*.

However, with the recent discovery of two Legion XXXIII denarius, we really need to rethink this theory and understand the propaganda purpose of this entire series.

If it was just to pay the troops, then a typical denarius promoting victory would have been sufficient. Even the denarii showing Antony and Octavian was to promote their alliance. They also issued these coins in gold, projecting the stability of the Second Triumvirate.

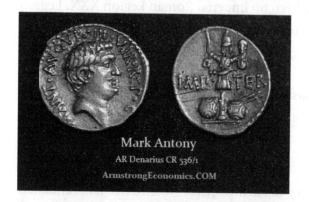

Mark Antony
AR Denarius CR 536/1
ArmstrongEconomics.COM

CR 517/2

Titus (79-81AD)
Opening of the Colosseum

ArmstrongEconomics.COM

Nero (54-68AD)
Opening of the Port of Ostia

The Romans used their coinage as ancient newspapers. The reverse would always announce some event, or at times, offer prayers to the gods. Here is a Roman bronze Sestertius announcing the opening of the Colosseum and announcing the opening of the Port of Ostia to receive grain.

Titus Pompeii Eruption Vesuvius
Atonement Denarii Series
of 79AD
Praying to avert further catastrophes

Jupiter

Neptune

Apollo

Former Emperors

ArmstrongEconomics.COM

Titus devoted much of his silver coinage of atonement to the gods for the disaster of Pompeii. There were four main atonement issues commemorating the services of prayer and propitiation through which the emperor attempted to address the public alarm over the disaster. People often attributed such events to the gods being angry. The coinage showed emblems seeking the approval of Jupiter, Neptune, Apollo, and the deceased former emperors to watch over the Roman people.

Tiberius (14-37 AD) issued this sestertius, announcing relief for Asia when a major earthquake devastated the region. This was modern-day Turkey. This region is prone to these major DOUBLE earthquakes. There was a major earthquake in 17 AD resulting in a financial panic in ancient Rome. Emperor

Tiberius (14-37AD)
AE Sestertius, struck 22-23AD (27.8 grams)
CIVITATIBVS ASIAE RESTITVTIS
In 17AD, the city of Sades was hit by a major earthquake.
Tiberius waived all taxes for 5 years & donated 10 million sesterces
ArmstrongEconomics.COM

Tiberius issued these coins, noting that they were for the relief of that region, Asia. He also suspended all taxation in the region. Even since, there have been eighty-one such major earthquakes.

Hadrian's cancelled all debts and burned promissory notes owed in a general amnesty for tax arrears

Here is also a Roman bronze sestertius of Hadrian (117-138 AD) announcing a tax amnesty cancelling all debts in taxes owed to the state. Once again, just as Tiberius suspended taxation allowing the people to recover in Asia, here we have Hadrian forgiving back taxes. Never have we witnessed any government claiming to be socialist cancelling taxes. That is something they would NEVER do these days.

You even have Roman Emperors such as Trajan (98-117 AD) engaging in social legislation known as the Alimenta, which was a welfare program that helped orphans and poor children throughout Italy. The Alimenta provided general funds, food, and subsidized education for children. The funding came from the Dacian War booty initially. When that ran out, it was funded by a combination of estate taxes and philanthropy. The state provided loans like Fannie Mae providing mortgages on Italian farms (fundi). The registered landowners in Italy received a lump sum from the imperial treasury and in return the interest paid funded the program.

Trajan. AD 98-117
AU Aureus (18mm, 7.18 g)
Rome mint. Struck 111AD Trajan extending right hand towards boy and girl

Trebonianus Gallus
(251-253AD)
The invading Goths from the East brought a devastating outbreak of plague
This Antoninianus struck at Rome in 253 AD displays on its reverse
"APOLL SALVTARI" Apollo Salutaris standing left, with olive branch and lyre
resting upon rock in his role as healer (Salutaris). It claimed the life of co-emperor
Hostilian. This plea to Apollo on the Roman coinage was the because of the plague

This coin was issued by Trebonianus Gallus (251-253 AD), appealing to Apollo Salutaris, who was believed to have been the god of healing. The Plague of Cyprian infected the Roman Empire from about 249 to 262 AD. It takes its name from St. Cyprian, who was the bishop of Carthage. He was a historian who witnessed and described the plague. It is not known precisely what this plague was. However, from the description, it may have been smallpox, measles, or a viral hemorrhagic fever like the Ebola virus.

The plague weakened Rome during the third century, causing a widespread decline in the workforce. That resulted in food shortages due to a lack of manpower to produce food for the Roman army. This contributed greatly to the collapse of the third century.

As you can see, Roman coins were ancient newspapers in coin form. The purpose of the legionary denarii of Mark Antony and Cleopatra was intimidation and propaganda. This was the wealth of Egypt on display as well. Otherwise, a single denarius proclaiming the gods were with them should have been efficient, as here with Fortuna promising good fortune.

Mark Antony (83 - 30BC)
AR Denarius (struck 42 BC) Rome mint;
(Bare head right, wearing short beard / Fortuna standing left)
C. Vibius Varus, moneyer - Crawford 494/32
ArmstrongEconomics.COM

This pair were sold as fake by Numismatica Ars Classica NAC AG. A closer look reveals an engraving alteration. This also applies to the coins illustrated by E. J. Haeberlin. This opens the question of engraver errors, intending XX rather than XXX, or if they were intentionally for propaganda purposes and handed to senators.

Counterfeiters' Die of Mark Antony
Iron die for AR Denarius Legionary issue
Legion VI
Classical Numismatic Group Auction 109
September 12, 2018 Lot number: 750

Remarkably, there has been one original die that has survived. Here is a counterfeiter's die as well. Ancient forgers were not very competent. There was also the possibility that when Antony lost, dies could have been seized and sold on the black market. There was no guarantee that one would even have a complete set of obverse and reverse together.

MARK ANTONY Legionary Die Circa 32 BC
Obverse die, bronze within iron sheath, for a Legionary Denarius
Dimensions: length, 26mm; width, 24mm, weight: 57.61 grams
Incuse - ANT. AVG. III VIR. R. P. C, galley to the right

Nero Claudius Drusus Fourrée Denarius
Silver plating breaking down over copper core
hence the Frech word for "stuffed" with copper
This coin is not genuinely known with this
obverse/reverse combination.
They used the Reverse of another coin

ArmstrongEconomics.COM

It has long been suspected that counterfeiters may have had some help from people in the minting process, for some of their forgeries were well-executed in style. They would typically take a copper core, overlay it with a thin sheet of silver, and strike the coin, fusing the two together. This is why you will often find a small punch mark, which is a banker's test looking for counterfeit *Fourrée* denarii.

Mark Antony XIX Legionary Denarius

Counterfeit AR Fourrée Legionary Denarius
Local or Geto-Dacian Imitation (2.65 grams)

Genuine Legionary Denarius
Silver (3.9 grams)

This is an example of a forger's attempt to imitate the legionary denarius. The wording is not quite right, and the design appears less defined.

Legion XXXIII Denarii

IN 43 BCE, SERVIUS Sulpicius Galba, one of the assassins of Julius Caesar, wrote a letter to Cicero in which he noted that Antony had commanded a Thirty-Fifth Legion at the Battle of Mutina in April of that year (Sulpicius went on to claim that he himself put the Thirty-Fifth Legion to flight at the beginning of the battle.). Antony's Thirty-Firth Legion is otherwise completely unknown to history, and there is no documented record of Antony having in his service at Actium or anywhere else a legion numbered higher than the Twenty-Third Legion.

There have been a few modern-day reports of legionary denarii for legions numbered XXIV through XXX, but it has been assumed that these are forgeries (perhaps by Tardani), or the result of errors on the part of the die engravers.

This changed on March 23, 2017, when the legionary denarius shown above for the Thirty-Third Legion sold at auction for £4,400 (equivalent to $5,507 at the time). Although there is a slight die shift on the reverse, the coin clearly references an otherwise unknown Thirty-Third Legion. The coin appears to be genuine: its style, metal composition, weight, thickness, and all other aspects are consistent with other legionary denarii that are unquestionably authentic. A second example of the Thirty-Third Legion denarius sold at auction in January 2022 for $52,000 against a $2,000 estimate. The market seems to have accepted these coins as authentic.

There is a possibility that the Legio XXXIII coins are both authentic. This has raised two possibilities. First, that there may well never have been a Thirty-Third Legion in Antony's army, but at the same time Antony may have ordered his moneyers to strike coins in the name of this nonexistent legion (and perhaps other nonexistent legions), in order to make it appear that his army was much larger than it actually was.

Others have argued that both Legion XXXIII specimens are from same dies. They concede that they are genuine, but they might be an engraver error of XXXIII instead of XXIII. They further argue that the existence of these two specimens does not confirm that Antony had legion XXXIII.

It was often considered, wrongly, that coins with a legion greater than LEG XXIII were fakes. The entire purpose of this series was intimidation and to proclaim Antony had the overwhelming support of the legions. This was simply Antony's strategy to project that his forces were far greater than those of Octavian.

Antony's coinage has surfaced noting: XXIV, XXV, XXVI, XXVII, XXVIII, XXIX, and XXX. Antony is known to have commanded a Legio XXXV at the Battle of Mutina; in a remarkable passage in Servius Sulpicius Galba's 43 BC letter to Cicero we are provided with the only surviving evidence for this legion's existence:

> *"on the 15th of April, the day on which Pansa was to arrive at the camp of Hirtius, with the former of whom I was – for I had gone along the road a hundred miles to hasten his arrival – Antony brought out two legions, the second and the thirty-fifth, and two praetorian cohorts...."*

(Epistulae ad Familiares 10.30)

Therefore, the existence of legions in the service of Antony with numbers greater than XXIII which have escaped the notice of history is entirely possible. Many of his units were never at full strength, and some may have effectively marched only on paper for propaganda purposes to intimidate Octavian. This is by far the rarest of the legionary denarii of Mark Antony. There are only two surviving examples which are clearly genuine examples, unambiguously inscribed LEG XXXIII.

Restitution Legion XVI Denarii

MARCUS AURELIUS. AR "Legionary" Denarius Restitution
Commemorative issued 168 AD commemorating the 200th annversary
of the battle of Actium (3.60 gm)

ArmstrongEconomics.COM

ARCUS AURELIUS (161-180 AD) and Lucius Verus (161-169 AD) issued a commemorative probably in 168 AD which was the 200th Anniversary of the Battle of Actium. This restoration issue demonstrates just how significant they remained in the memory of the Romans, even 200 years later. It certainly marked the birth of Imperial Rome, the defeat of Cleopatra's proxy war, and "restored" Antony's legionary denarii.

This restoration has been investigated extensively by Martin Beckmann.[8] It consists of a series of denarii appearing to copy those of Antony, including the legends of the original coins.

However, they added an inscription ANTONINVS ET VERVS AVG(usti) REST(ituerunt), "Antoninus and Verus, Augusti, restored (this coin)." These restorations have been described as "exactly copied from the original" but close examination shows that this is not the case. Their purpose has been debated, with a tendency to focus on the fact that the only legion named on these restored coins is the sixth and from this infer a commemorative function relevant to this legion.

---

8   *The Restoration of Mark Antony's Legionary Denarii* by Marcus Aurelius and Lucius Verus, 2017, Numismatic Chronicle 2017

Collecting Legionary Denarii

Antony's Legionary Denarii Set

ArmstrongEconomics.COM

DESPITE THE FACT that Cleopatra's proxy war using Antony to divide and conquer Rome failed, the number of legionary denarii struck was enormous with a total mintage of 25 million to 35 million coins, accounting for 20% of the money supply even 100 years later based on the finds in Pompeii.[9] Many of the surviving specimens are extremely worn and most were probably melted down and reused by other emperors during the Imperial period.

---

9   Woytek, B. "Die Münzen der römischen Republik unter der Übergangszeit zum Prinzipat im Museum Carnuntinum," *Numismata Carnuntina* (Alram, M. and Schmidt-Dick, F., *eds.*). Forschungen under Material. Vienna. (2007)

LEG IIII   LEG IIX   LEG VIIII

The Delos Hoard discovered in 1905, containing 604 specimens, indicated that Legion II was the most common, with Legions V and VI not far behind. The three rarest were Legion IIII, IIX, and XVIIII.

Antony's legionary denarii were by far the absolute largest issue of silver coinage ever produced during the Roman Republican period and into the early Imperial era. The third-century Roman historian, Cassius Dio (Roman History 50.18.2), had confirmed that Antony was better funded than Octavian. That was simply because his funding was all from Cleopatra since this was her proxy war to conquer Rome. As I have mentioned, about 20% of all the coins discovered in Pompeii, which was buried in 79AD, some 110 years later, further confirms Cassius Dio's comments.

Octavian did not seize and melt down the legionary denarii. He perhaps viewed them as the spoils and apparently used then to pay his own soldiers in the aftermath of the Battle of Actium.

The Delos Hoard was unearthed during the excavations of the French School in a house near the theater on Delos. It consisted of 604 coins of Antony's legions out of 650 in total. There was one of Juba I of Numidia, while the rest were Roman denarii. The Roman coinage can be divided into two groups. The first was with Roman Republic denarii with 604 coins of Antony's legionary denarii.

Juba I of Numidia
(c.85–46 BC)
King of Numidia modern day Algeria
ArmstrongEconomics.COM

There was also a smaller portion of earlier Roman Republican denarii dated from 147 BC to 40 BC. Therefore, this hoard clearly dates to the period of the Battle of Actium. The Delos hoard can also be compared with other finds from the Actium area itself and Euboea (Styrra), which show the same composition. Such hoards are rare in Greece (in total, four) and must be connected to the movements of Antony's army in the aftermath of the naval battle.

Hoard of Roman coins dating back to Mark Antony are discovered in Welsh field: 91 pieces of 2,000-year-old silver could be worth 'tens of thousands of pounds'

- The hoard of 91 coins was found in Wick, Wales by two walkers
- It has been declared treasure, but there is no official valuation yet
- Oldest coins date back to 31 BC and were issued by general Mark Antony
- Known for his relationship with Cleopatra and growth of Roman Empire

By SARAH GRIFFITHS FOR MAILONLINE
UPDATED: 11:05 EDT, 26 November 2015

The hoard of ninety-one coins was found in Wick, Wales, by two walkers in 2015 as reported by the *Daily Mail.* The coins spanned 200 years, with the earliest dating back to Mark Antony and 31 BC. It appears to have been buried during the reign of Marcus Aurelius, who headed the Empire from 161 AD to 180 AD.

There have been several hoards that contained Mark Antony's legionary denarii. The denarii discovered in Greece appear to have been from Roman soldiers and were probably spent in local trade.

There was the 2018 Norton Hoard[10] in Yorkshire, Britain, of 1,056 Roman silver coins, spanning approximately 192 years of Roman rule in Britain, which was discovered by a metal detector. The Norton Hoard contained coins from eighteen Roman Emperors, with the earliest coins of Mark Antony's legionary denarii. The last emperor was Severus Alexander (222-235 AD) and political turmoil erupted thereafter.

The denarii clearly circulated throughout the rest of the empire. The extent of circulation appears to have been up to the mid-first century AD and declined thereafter into the third century AD representing only a small portion of later hoards. They still were circulating in quantity in Britain immediately after the Roman conquest in 43 AD. Hoard evidence and contemporary references indicate that Antony's legionary denarii were still circulating during the reign of Severus Alexander (222-235 AD).

---

10   https://www.bbc.com/news/uk-england-south-yorkshire-65244111

The Shapwick Hoard - Consisting of 9,262 Roman Silver Denarii Coins

The Shapwick Hoard is one of the largest all-silver denarii ever uncovered. It was discovered in Somerset, England, in September 1998. This hoard contained 9,262 Roman coins and dates to after 224 AD. It still contained 260 legionary denarii (3% of the total hoard). The next earliest coins in that hoard were produced under Nero (54–68 AD). There is a huge gap between Nero of 54 AD and Antony's legionary denarii of 31 BC of 85 years, once again suggesting that sheer quantity issued by Antony and Cleopatra was indeed exceptional.

Shapwick Hoard

Reign	Date	Number in Hoard
Mark Antony	31 BC	260
Nero	54–68	44
Galba	68–69	12
Otho	69	9
Vitellius	69	30
Vespasian	69–79	548
Titus	79–81	69
Domitian	81–96	21
Nerva	96–98	12
Trajan	98–117	91
Hadrian	117–138	117
Antoninus Pius	138–161	567
Marcus Aurelius	161–180	171
Commodus	180–192	356
Septimius Severus	193–211	5,741
Caracalla	198–217	345
Macrinus	217–218	61
Elagabalus	218–222	688
Severus Alexander	222–235	120

Octavian, 44-27 BC
AR Denarius (3.98 grams), moving with military mint in Greece, autumn 42 BC
CAESAR - Helmeted Mars rt/S-C Trophy 2 standards
Crawford 497/3
ArmstrongEconomics.COM

Thousands of Antony's legionary denarii have survived in various conditions, remaining very popular among ancient coin collectors. Assembling a collection in high condition of extremely fine is a challenge, to say the least.

A survey of the discovered hoards from the late first century BC reveals once again that Antony's legionary denarii are far more commonly found than coins of Octavian. This applies even to the regions where veterans were given land on their retirement for services rendered, once more attesting to the sheer magnitude of Cleopatra's funding for this proxy war to conquer Rome.

The extensive quantity of Antony's legionary denarii issued played a role in the end of local minting of silver coinage in Greece and the Aegean Sea region for many years to come. Local communities seem to have only issued bronze provincial coinage for small transactions. Even looking at Cappadocia, in modern-day Turkey, we do not see silver coinage of any significance until about fifty-two years later during the reign of Tiberius (14-37 AD).

Octavian does not appear to have been melting the coinage down and re-striking it. Furthermore, Antony's slightly debased legionary denarii compared to Octavian's would have meant that after recoining, the number of denarii would have been less. That certainly would not have made it a profitable enterprise to melt

Cappadocia Caesarea-Eusebia
Tiberius with Drusus Caesar
(14-37AD)
AR Drachm
ArmstrongEconomics.COM

Antony's denarii down. It was far better to leave them in circulation, thereby not taking responsibility for the slight debasement.

It's possible that the debased silver content of Antony's legionary denarii ensured their survivability. As illustrated here, following the death of Nero in 68 AD, this is when we find denarii of Antony still in circulation, but counterstamped by Vespasian (69-79 AD) "**IMP VES,**" recertifying its validity rather than melting it down, which would not have been profitable.

Mark Antony Legionary Denarius (32-31BC)
Counterstamped ("IMP VES")
By Vespasian (69-79AD) during Post-Nero Civil War

ArmstrongEconomics.COM

Their low silver content meant that the Imperial government did not try to recall and remint them, as they did for other Republican and early Imperial coin issues. It also meant that they were not removed from circulation by the operation of Gresham's law, for they were debased.

In the year 107 AD, Emperor Trajan attempted to address the inflation unleashed by his Dacian War. He ordered that they "melted down all the worn-out coinage," according to the historian Cassius Dio. The treasury was depleted due to his prolonged campaign to conquer Dacia, in the former Yugoslavia region.

Trajan demonetized all silver and gold coinage that had been issued prior to the reign of Nero (54-68 AD) and his monetary reform of 64 AD, which was the first debasement to pay for the Great fire of Rome. Therefore, Trajan (98-117 AD) recalled all "worn" coinage, melting down and reducing the silver content from 93.5% to eventually 90% by 112 AD. What is interesting is that he replaced the old coinage with restitution issues, even Augustus's aureus with the crocodile announcing Egypt was captured. However, he did not issue any restored coinage of Antony's legionary denarii, for that was not profitable.

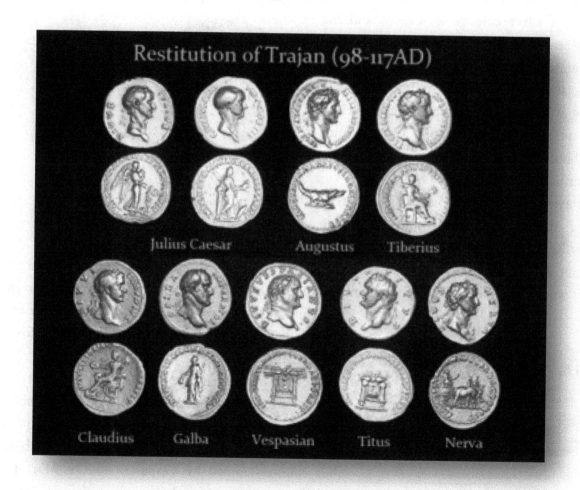

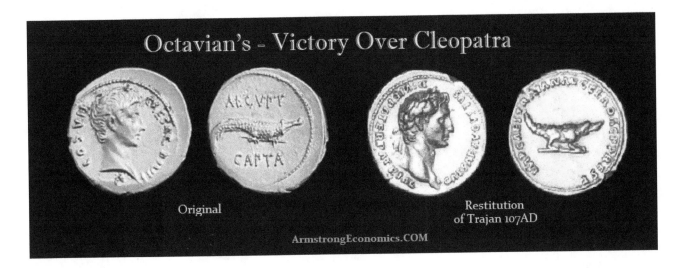

Octavian's - Victory Over Cleopatra

Original

Restitution
of Trajan 107AD

ArmstrongEconomics.COM

Consequently, Trajan demonetized the old coinage which was of a heavier silver and gold standard—meaning they were no longer valid payment for taxes. This forced people to return them in exchange for new denarii. European countries, prior to the euro, routinely canceled their currencies to force people to pay taxes. The old coin was then melted and in effect this increased the money supply by about 10%. The fact that the legionary denarii of Antony were omitted when they were still well more than 10% of the entire money supply by this point in time, confirms their debasement was not profitable to melt down.

Hoard evidence suggests that by the reign of Vespasian (69–79 AD), legionary denarii still made up around a 20% of all denarii in circulation in Asia. Highly worn examples continue to appear frequently in hoards into the third century AD.

Moreover, hoard evidence demonstrates that the legionary denarii continued to form a large part of the coinage in circulation in the Roman Imperial period and certainly peaked before time of Marcus Aurelius (161-180 AD). Looking at the Shapwick Hoard, another interesting fact emerges. The two most represented coins of emperors are that of Vespasian (69-79 AD) and Septimius Severus (193-211 AD). These are both emperors who prevailed during the civil war that followed Nero's death in 68 AD and Commodus (177-192 AD) who was assassinated in 192 AD. Once more, we see a sharp increase in the money supply during these two civil wars 124 years apart. Civil war was always costly.

Bibliography

Babelon, Earnest. *Description historique et chronologique des monnaies de la République romaine vulgairement appelées monnaies consulaires.* Paris: Rollin et Feuardent, 1885-1886.

Harl, Kenneth W. *Coinage in the Roman Economy, 300 B.C. to A.D. 700.* Baltimore: Johns Hopkins University Press, 1996.

Sear, David, R. *The History and Coinage of the Roman Imperators 49-27 BC.* London: SPINK, 1998.

Sydenham, Edward Allen, Geoffrey Colton Haines, L. Forrer, and Charles Austin Hersh. *The Coinage of the Roman Republic.* Rockville Centre, New York: Numismatic Publications, 1995.

Tullius Cicero, M. Letters of Cicero After the Death of Cæsar (S.H. Jeyes, transl.). Nabu Press. (2010 reprint)

Auction Houses

- Classical Numismatic Group, LLC (https://www.cngcoins.com)
- Roma Numismatics, Ltd (https://romanumismatics.com)
- Numismatica Ars Classica NAC AG (https://www.arsclassicacoins.com)
- Leu Numismatik AG (https://leunumismatik.com)
- Bertolami Fine Art (www.bertolamifineart.com)

Acknowledgment of Assistance in Research and Editing

Hannah Jackson
Cassandra D'Amelio
Giuliano Russo
Andrew McCabe